Series / Number 07-026

MULTIATTRIBUTE EVALUATION

WARD EDWARDS
J. ROBERT NEWMAN
Social Science Research Institute
University of Southern California

with the collaboration of

KURT SNAPPER
DAVID SEAVER
Maxima, Inc.
Bethesda, Maryland

SAGE PUBLICATIONS
The International Professional Publishers
Thousand Oaks   London   New Delhi

For information:

SAGE Publications, Inc.
2455 Teller Road
Thousand Oaks, California 91320
E-mail: order@sagepub.com

SAGE Publications Ltd.
6 Bonhill Street
London EC2A 4PU
United Kingdom

SAGE Publications India Pvt. Ltd.
M-32 Market
Greater Kailash I
New Delhi 110 048 India

Printed in the United States of America

International Standard Book Number 0-8039-0095-3

Library of Congress Catalog Card No. L.C. 82-040334

This book is printed on acid-free paper.

98 99 00 01 02 03 14 13 12 11 10 9 8 7 6

When citing a university paper, please use the proper form. Remember to cite the Sage University Paper series title and incude the paper number. One of the following formats can be adapted (depending on the style manual used):

(1) EDWARDS, W., and NEWMAN, J. R. (1982). "Multiattribute Evaluation." Sage University Papers Series on Quantitative Applications in the Social Sciences, 07-026. Beverly Hills, CA: Sage.

OR

(2) Edwards, W., & Newman, J. R. (1982). *Multiattribute evaluation.* (Sage University Papers Series on Quantitative Application in the Social Sciences, series no. 07-026). Beverly Hills, CA: Sage.

CONTENTS

SERIES EDITOR'S INTRODUCTION

Program evaluation, in the words of the authors of this new addition to our series, is "rapidly becoming big business." Those who sponsor programs, and especially those who pay for them, want to know whether the programs are worthwhile. This is true of small-scale, one-time-only projects as well as of expensive, large-scale, continuous projects. In *Multiattribute Evaluation,* Ward Edwards and J. Robert Newman, with Kurt Snapper and David Seaver-all experienced analysts-describe a method of evaluation known as Multiattribute Utility Technology. Despite the forbidding title, the approach is rather simple and straight forward. The heart of the procedure is that it requires representatives of the program to identify the most relevant values or attributes that are a part of the program. Measurements are then made to determine the degree to which these attributes are attained. By doing so systematically, and by making judgments numerical whenever possible, decisions can be made on a more precise and objective basis than is often the case.

Although readers may initially find the terminology unfamiliar, they will find the monograph very clearly written. Both real and hypothetical examples are used throughout to clarify all of the points. And while the method is rigorous, only elementary mathematics is required.

Multiattribute Evaluation should be useful to individuals across a wide variety of disciplines, since evaluation work knows no traditional disciplinary bounds. The monograph is helpful in this regard since examples are drawn from several areas. Even those familiar with other forms of evaluation will find it a stimulating discussion of one appropriate way to go about a rigorous, quantitative assessment of social programs.

—*Richard G. Niemi*
Series Co-Editor

MULTIATTRIBUTE EVALUATION

WARD EDWARDS
J. ROBERT NEWMAN
Social Science Research Institute
University of Southern California

with the collaboration of

KURT SNAPPER
DAVID SEAVER
Maxima, Inc.
Bethesda, Maryland

1. EVALUATION OF SOCIAL PROGRAMS

Evaluation is rapidly becoming Big Business. Questions like "Is this plan wise?" "Should I choose option A or option B?" "At what funding level should this program be supported?" How well is this program doing?" have been asked of social programs since long before we were born. But the idea that one could answer such questions systematically and in a manner other than simply looking at the object of evaluation and making an intuitive judgment is a development of the 1960s and 1970s. As inflated costs and less-inflated program budgets come into steadily escalating conflict, the task of weeding out the programs worthy of support from those that are not, and of providing guidance for programs in existence, will continue to grow in importance—as will the resources and attention devoted to developing satisfying methods of performing that task.

What Is Evaluation?

The literature of evaluation is already huge, and grows daily. The purpose of this paper is not academic, and we do not intend more than the

AUTHORS' NOTE: *This paper was developed under a grant from the National Institute of Law Enforcement and Criminal Justice, Law Enforcement Assistance Administration, Department of Justice (LEAA Grant No. 79-NI-AX-0002). Points of view or opinions stated in this document are those of the authors and do not necessarily represent the official position or policies of the U.S. Department of Justice.*

7

most cursory of references even to the literature on the method of evaluation that is our topic. For a recent and very scholarly presentation of evaluation methods and results from a broad spectrum of viewpoints, including our own, see Klein and Teilmann (1980). Edwards's chapter in that book will be of particular interest to scholars who find the ideas presented in this paper stimulating and potentially useful to them, since it discusses the same ideas in a far more technical way, reviews a significant amount of literature, and cites the literature of this and of other methods.

The purpose of this paper is to present one approach to evaluation: Multiattribute Utility Technology (MAUT). We have attempted to make a version of MAUT simple and straightforward enough so that the reader can, with diligence and frequent reexaminations of it, conduct relatively straightforward MAUT evaluations him- or herself. In so doing, we will frequently resort to techniques that professional decision analysts will recognize as approximations and/or assumptions. The literature justifying those approximations is extensive and complex; to review it here would blow to smithereens our goal of being nontechnical.

What is MAUT, and how does it relate to other approaches to evaluation? Edwards, Guttentag, and Snapper (1975) discussed that question in 1975, and we have little to add. MAUT depends on a few key ideas:

(1) When possible, evaluations should be comparative.
(2) Programs normally serve multiple constituencies.
(3) Programs normally have multiple goals, not all equally important.
(4) Judgments are inevitably a part of any evaluation.
(5) Judgments of magnitude are best when made numerically.
(6) Evaluations typically are, or at least should be, relevant to decisions.

Some of the six points above are less innocent than they seem. If programs serve multiple constituencies, evaluations of them should normally be addressed to the interests of those constituencies; different constituencies can be expected to have different interests. If programs have multiple goals, evaluations should attempt to assess how well they serve them; this implies multiple measures and comparisons. The task of dealing with multiple measures of effectiveness (which may well be simple subjective judgments in numerical form) makes less appealing the notion of social programs as experiments or quasi-experiments. While the tradition that programs should be thought of as experiments, or at least as quasi experiments, has wide currency and wide appeal in evaluation research, its implementation becomes more difficult as the number of measures needed for a satisfactory evaluation increases. When experimental or other hard data are available, they can easily be incorporated in a MAUT evaluation.

Finally, the willingness to accept subjectivity into evaluation, combined with the insistence that judgments be numerical, serves several useful purposes. First, it partly closes the gap between intuitive and judgmental evaluations and the more quantitative kind; indeed, it makes coexistence of judgment and objective measurement within the same evaluation easy and natural. Second, it opens the door to easy combination of complex concatenations of values. For instance, evaluation researchers often distinguish between process evaluations and outcome evaluations. Process and outcome are different, but if a program has goals of both kinds, its evaluation can and should assess its performance on both. Third, use of subjective inputs can, if need be, greatly shorten the time required for an evaluation to be carried out. A MAUT evaluation can be carried out from original definition of the evaluation problem to preparation of the evaluation report in as little as a week of concentrated effort. The inputs to such an abbreviated evaluative activity will obviously be almost entirely subjective. But the MAUT technique at least produces an audit trail such that the skeptic can substitute other judgments for those that seem doubtful, and can then examine what the consequences for the evaluation are. We know of no MAUT social program evaluation that took less than two months, but in some other areas of application we have participated in execution of complete MAUT evaluations in as little as two days—and then watched them be used as the justification for major decisions. Moreover, we heartily approved; time constraints on the decision made haste necessary, and we were very pleased to have the chance to provide some orderly basis for decision in so short a time.

Classes of Purposes for Evaluations

Evaluations can be done for various reasons; different reasons can and do lead to different forms of evaluative activities. The most common reason for evaluation is that it is required; perhaps by mandate from Congress or from a sponsor or perhaps by rules internal to the program organization.

The organizational requirement for an evaluation is normally based on the supposition that decisions need to be made. Sometimes the question is whether the program should be continued, modified, or scrapped. Sometimes it is simply what relatively minor changes, if any, should be made in program design, management, or functioning to improve its effectiveness. Sometimes no specific decisions are behind such mandated evaluations; the spirit of such evaluations is somewhat similar to the spirit that leads to annual external audit of corporate books.

Major evaluations are often required as a basis for potential major programmatic changes—up to and including the most major of all changes: the birth or death of a program. Sometimes such decisions are pure life-or-death choices; at least equally often, some social problem requires attention, and the decision problem is which of several alternative approaches to dealing with it looks most promising. Funding-level decisions are also programmatic choices; the same program at two substantially different funding levels is really two different programs.

From this welter of considerations, we think we can distinguish four different classes of reasons for evaluations: curiosity, monitoring, fine tuning, and programmatic choice. Curiosity in itself is seldom a basis for wisely performed evaluations, since most programs are too specific in character for the kinds of generalizations to which wisely applied curiosity can lead, and generalized curiosity is a poor guide to choice of evaluative methods or measures.

Monitoring is both an appropriate and a necessary function for any program, and we believe MAUT offers useful tools for monitoring. Monitoring shades over into fine tuning; the same tools are relevant to both. Programmatic choice is the most important use to which evaluative information can be put, and the tools of MAUT are most directly relevant to it.

These reasons for evaluation share two common characteristics that make MAUT applicable to them all. The first is that, implicitly or explicitly, all require comparison of something with something else. This is most obvious in the case of programmatic choice. But even monitoring has the characteristic, since one normally wonders whether or not some minor change would change significantly one of the monitored values. An important implication of the comparative nature of virtually every evaluation is that some of the comparisons are inevitably between the program as it is and the program as it might be—that is, between real and imaginary programs or programmatic methods. The necessity of comparing real with imaginary objects is one of the problems that most approaches to evaluation find very difficult to solve. The normal approach of traditional methods is to make the comparison object real, typically by embodying it in an experimental (or control) group, locus, or program. We admire such comparisons when they can be made (e.g., in drug trials), but consider them impractical for most social program evaluations. MAUT deals with this problem by accepting data and judgments on equivalent footings; judgment is the most generally useful tool we know of for assessing the consequences of nonexistent programs. (Such judgments, of course, are best when based on relevant data, e.g., from other programs in other places.)

The second characteristic that the various reasons for evaluation share is that programs virtually always have multiple objectives; consequently, evaluations should assess as many of these as seem important.

We use the word "program" in a broader sense than has been common; we are concerned with many social programs other than social service delivery programs. We consider arms procurement, treaties among nations, labor contracts, choices made by businesses about such questions as where to locate new plants, and other similar public decisions with major impacts on people to be "programs," and to deserve evaluation. One version or another of the methods we discuss has been used for purposes as diverse as deciding whether to expand a Community Anti-Crime Program area, evaluating the Office of the Rentalsman in Vancouver as a dispute resolution mechanism, evaluating alternative school desegregation plans for Los Angeles, choosing among alternative sites for dams and nuclear power plants, evaluating competing bids for various kinds of military hardware, formulating U.S. negotiating positions in international negotiations, and assessing the combat readiness of Marine Corps brigades. For more information and a number of references to such applications, see Edwards (1980).

Since we claim that MAUT can be applied to evaluative problems of each of the kinds we can identify, are we asserting that it is a universally applicable mode of evaluation—perhaps a substitute for alternative modes? No. MAUT is, we believe, a very widely applicable method of organizing and presenting evaluative information. As such, it is compatible with any other evaluative activity designed to yield numbers as outputs. Since the ideas of MAUT do not limit the sources of the evaluative information, they can be combined with whatever data sources the evaluator finds satisfying and relevant to his or her problem.

Is MAUT an evaluative method at all? Without an answer to the question about where the evaluative information it must use will come from, the answer is no. However, chapter 6 of this paper presents some ideas about answers to that question. Whether those answers are a part of MAUT or external to it is obviously only a question of definition; the reader can choose.

Steps in a MAUT Evaluation

It may be helpful at this point to summarize concisely the steps involved in any MAUT evaluation. This will (1) summarize the remainder of this paper; (2) provide a brief procedural guide; and (3) identify, but not define, the technical terms (they are defined one by one in the remainder of the paper).

First, a note about technical terms. There are a lot of them, and many will seem nonstandard to those familiar with the MAUT literature. In every case that we can identify, use of a nonstandard term corresponds to a shading of difference between what this paper discusses and what previous publications (including many of which Edwards was an author) have discussed. Many more versions of MAUT exist than researchers active in developing it. While all depend on the same basic ideas, details of implementation change, and such changes produce corresponding changes in jargon. Many nontechnical readers will wish to skip this section and go on to the next.

Step 1. Identify the objects of evaluation and the function or functions that the evaluation is intended to perform. Normally there will be several objects of evaluation, at least some of them imaginary, since evaluations are comparative. The functions of the evaluation will often control the choice of objects of evaluation. We have argued that evaluations should help decision makers to make decisions. If the nature of those decisions is known, the objects of evaluation will often be controlled by that knowledge. Step I is outside the scope of this paper. Some of the issues inherent in it have already been discussed in this chapter. Chapter 2, devoted to setting up an example that will be carried through the document, illustrates Step I for that example.

Step 2. Identify the *stakeholders* (technical terms to be explained later are set in italics). Chapter 3 discusses this in detail.

Step 3. Elicit from stakeholder representatives the relevant *value dimensions or attributes,* and (often) organize them into a hierarchical structure called a *value tree.* Chapter 3 both explains how to do this and presents several real examples.

Step 4. Assess for each stakeholder group the *relative importance of* each of the values identified at Step 3. Such judgments can, of course, be expected to vary from one stakeholder group to another; methods of dealing with such value conflicts are important. Chapter 4 presents assessment techniques and introduces some discussion of value differences. Chapter 7 returns to the issue of value differences.

Step 5. Ascertain how well each object of evaluation serves each value at the lowest level of the value tree. Such numbers, called *single-attribute utilities or location measures,* ideally report measurements, expert judgments, or both. If so, they should be independent of stakeholders and so of value disagreements among stakeholders; however, this ideal is not always met. Location measures need to be on a common scale, in order for Step 4 to make sense. Chapter 5, which is so far as we know unique in this literature in its emphasis on simplicity of methods, discusses both how to obtain location measures and how to put them on a common scale.

Step 6. Aggregate location measures with measures of importance. This is the topic of chapter 6.

Step 7. Perform *sensitivity analyses.* The question underlying any sensitivity analysis is whether a change in the analysis, e.g., using different numbers as inputs, will lead to different conclusions. While conclusions may have emerged from Step 6, they deserve credence as a basis for action only after their sensitivity is explored in Step 7. Chapter 7 shows how some fairly simple sensitivity analyses can be performed.

Steps 6 and 7 will normally produce the results of a MAUT evaluation. Chapter 7 also has suggestions about how such results can be presented.

The Relation Between Evaluation and Decision

The tools of MAUT are most useful for guiding decisions; they grow out of a broader methodological field called decision analysis. The relation of evaluation to decision has been a topic of debate among evaluation researchers—especially the academic evaluation researchers who wonder whether or not their evaluations are used, and if so, appropriately used. Some evaluators take the position that their responsibility is to provide the relevant facts; it is up to someone else to make the decisions. "We are not elected officials." This position is sometimes inevitable, of course; the evaluator is not the decision maker as a rule, and cannot compel the decision maker to attend to the result of the evaluation, or to base decisions on it. But it is unattractive to many evaluators; certainly to us.

We know of three devices that make evaluations more likely to be used in decisions. The first and most important is to involve the decision makers heavily in the evaluative process; this is natural if, as is normally the case, they are among the most important stakeholders. The second is to make the evaluation as directly relevant to the decision as possible, prefer ably by making sure that the options available to the decision maker are the objects of evaluation. The third is to make the product of the evaluation useful—which primarily means making it readable and short. Exhaustive scholarly documents tend to turn busy decision makers off. Of course, nothing in these obvious devices guarantees success in making the evaluation relevant to the decision. However, nonuse of these devices comes close to guaranteeing failure.

By "decisions" we do not necessarily mean anything apocalyptic; the process of fine tuning a program requires decisions too. This paper unabashedly assumes that either the evaluator or the person or organization commissioning the evaluation has the options or alternative courses of action in mind, and proposes to select among them in part on the basis of the evaluation—or else that the information is being assembled and aggregated because of someone's expectation that that will be the case later on.

TABLE 1
MKDC CAC Value Attributes

Number	Title of Attribute	Importance Weight
1	Reduce Crime	.141
2	Reduce Fear of Crime	.140
3	Increase Police Responsiveness	.119
4	Serve Community Ombudsman Role	.126
5	Increase Resident Involvement	.149 .111
6	Institutionalize Organization	.104
7	Provide Technical Assistance	.110
8	Integrate Other Social Services	1.000

An Example of a MAUT Analysis

The Office of Community Anti-Crime Programs (OCAP) of the Law Enforcement Assistance Administration (LEAA) funded a number of community-based anticrime projects throughout the country. Decision Science Consortium, Inc. was hired to perform a large MAUT analysis of this whole program; the key people in that evaluation were Dr. Kurt Snapper and Dr. David Seaver. A more detailed discussion of the evaluation as a whole appears in Chapter 3 of this paper.

The following discussion of a specific decision within that evaluation program is condensed from Snapper and Seaver (1978). One of the community projects within OCAP's program was that of the Midwood-Kings Highway Development Corporation (MKDC) in Brooklyn. The objectives (called *attributes* in this paper) of that particular project, and the *weights* given to them by its director, are given in Table 1. Note that all attributes are approximately equally important—a quite unusual finding. These attributes and weights were elicited in the first year of the MKDC project. The project was quite successful in improving on the preproject scores on these objectives in its area.[1]

In 1979, a decision problem arose. The City of New York adopted a "coterminality" policy; police and other service delivery areas were to become aligned or "coterminous" with community districts. Since MKDC served a part of the area served by the Midwood Civic Action Council (MCAC), the problem was whether to expand MKDC's area of service to include all of MCAC's area—a 50% expansion. No additional LEAA funds were expected for MKDC, so the concern was that expansion of the service area would lead to dilution of service quality and effectiveness. On

TABLE 2
A MAUT Analysis of the MKDC Expansion Decision

Value Attributes	1979	1980	1981
Option 1: Expand to include all the MCAC area			
1. Reduce Crime	68	78	85
2. Reduce Fear of Crime	43	64	90
3. Increase Police Responsiveness	63	83	98
4. Serve Ombudsman Role	25	42	83
5. Increase Resident Involvement	28	69	95
6. Institutionalize Organization	46	70	105
7. Give Technical Assistance	25	40	80
8. Integrate Social Services	75	88	97
Aggregate Utility	46	67	92
Option 2: Do not expand at all			
1. Reduce Crime	68	81	89
2. Reduce Fear of Crime	43	71	97
3. Increase Police Responsiveness	63	84	100
4. Serve Ombudsman Role	25	50	100
5. Increase Resident Involvement	28	85	100
6. Institutionalize Organization	46	66	100
7. Give Technical Assistance	25	50	100
8. Integrate Social Services	75	90	100
Aggregate Utility	46	73	98

the other hand, political considerations of various sorts argued for the expansion.

Working with Dr. Seaver and Dr. Snapper, the MKDC project director did a MAUT analysis of the two extreme options: to expand or not. The results are presented in Table 2. It is important to note that the measures on which Table 2 are based are judgments of the MKDC project director, and refer to the MKDC area alone. The baseline or *zero point* on each attribute is pre-MKDC project measures. The *100 point* on each dimension is the project director's judgment of the best that could be expected to be accomplished by the project. The weights used to combine the various utilities on each attribute into aggregate utilities come from Table 1. The aggregate utility serves as one basis for the evaluation—the higher these

TABLE 3
Project Effectiveness in the Full MCAC Area, Assuming Expansion

Value	Attributes	1979	1980	1981
1.	Reduce Crime	–5	63	76
2.	Reduce Fear of Crime	10	53	81
3.	Increase Police Responsiveness	0	63	84
4.	Serve Ombudsman Role	10	35	60
5.	Increase Resident Involvement	15	43	90
6.	Institutionalize Organization	NA	66	70
7.	Give Technical Assistance	0	25	50
8.	Integrate Social Services	0	75	90
	Aggregate Utility	5	53	76

values, the better the option. Note that both are sets of judgments by the project director. A less abbreviated MAUT would have included other stakeholders.

The project director was relatively surprised by the results presented in Table 2; he had expected that expansion of the service area would lead to much more degradation of service than Table 2 shows. He therefore chose to go ahead and expand the area, since he felt that in the presence of such a relatively minor effect on service, the political considerations were compelling.

Political events in New York City have delayed implementation of coterminality, and there is some doubt about whether it will ever be implemented. However, MKDC is now considering petitioning LEAA to expand its target area to all of MCAC's area.

One reason for that decision is yet another version of the analysis. Recall that Table 2 is based only on predicted measures within the original MKDC area. If the area were to be expanded, it would be appropriate to take those measures over the whole MCAC area instead. Table 3 shows the result of a MAUT analysis based on predicted measures covering the whole MCAC area. Note that expansion of the area leads to severe initial degradation (for the year 1979) of the project effectiveness measures, since the new area includes a substantial region within which the old MKDC project, which had been very successful, had not been operating. However, the forecast leads to the conclusion that, although the figures are not as high as either of those in MKDC alone, they show major improvement with time. This invites the idea that "the greatest good of the greatest number" is well served by expanding, even in the presence of constant funding.

The director also judged that a funding difference of only $60,000 would make the difference between leaving the original MKDC project ineffectual and giving it the necessary resources to serve all of the MCAC area as well as it was then serving MKDC. This is obviously an interesting assessment to report to LEAA in connection with any application to expand the MKDC area.

This is an example of a MAUT analysis carried out in a day. In spite of its brevity and omissions (e.g., of other stakeholders and of assessments of the political consequences of expanding or not expanding the area) it led a decision maker in a criminal justice project to change his mind, and provided him with the necessary information and analysis to defend that change of mind to sponsors, peers, and those he serves.

Summary

Chapter 1 begins by defining the purpose of the paper: to present a version of Multiattribute Utility Technology (MAUT). The version chosen for presentation emphasizes multiple stakeholders, multiple program objectives, wholehearted acceptance of subjectivity, and linkage of evaluation to decision. The chapter distinguished four reasons for evaluation: curiosity, monitoring, fine tuning, and several forms of programmatic choice. MAUT is useful to them all because it implies comparison of something with something else with respect to multiple objectives. MAUT is not a mode of evaluation in itself, instead, it is a way of organizing and aggregating evaluative efforts. The chapter briefly lists the seven steps of a MAUT, discusses the relationship between evaluation and decision, and makes suggestions about how evaluative efforts can be made more likely to influence decisions. It concludes with an instance of a MAUT evaluation that led to a decision.

2. AN EXAMPLE

In this chapter we present a fairly simple example of how to use multiattribute utility technology for evaluation. The example is intended to be simple enough to be understandable, yet complex enough to illustrate all of the technical ideas necessary for the analysis. Every idea introduced and illustrated is discussed in more detail in subsequent chapters. The example itself also reappears in later chapters.

Unfortunately, we cannot structure our discussion around the real example that we presented in the last chapter. It does not have all of the features of MAUT that we need to examine. So we have invented an example that brings out all the properties of the method, and that will, we hope, be sufficiently realistic to fit with the intuitions of those who work in a social program environment.

The Problem: How to Evaluate New Locations
for a Drug Counseling Center

The Drug-Free Center is a private nonprofit contract center that gives counseling to clients sent to it by the courts of its city as a condition of their probation. It is a walk-in facility with no beds or other special space requirements; it does not use methadone. It has just lost its lease, and must relocate.

The director of the center has screened the available spaces to which it might move. All spaces that are inappropriate because of zoning, excessive neighborhood resistance to the presence of the center, or inability to satisfy such legal requirements as access for the handicapped have been eliminated, as have spaces of the wrong size, price, or location. The city is in a period of economic recession, and so even after this prescreening a substantial number of options are available. Six sites are chosen as a result of informal screening for serious evaluation. The director must, of course, satisfy the sponsor, the probation department, and the courts that the new location is appropriate, and must take the needs and wishes of both employees and clients into account. But as a first cut, the director wishes simply to evaluate the sites on the basis of values and judgments of importance that make sense internally to the center.

The Evaluation Process

The first task is to identify stakeholders. They were listed in the previous paragraph. A stakeholder is simply an individual or group with a reason to care about the decision and with enough impact on the decision maker so that the reason should be taken seriously. Stakeholders are sources of *value attributes.* An attribute is something that the stakeholders, or some subset of them, care about enough so that failure to consider it in the decision would lead to a poor decision. We discuss the elicitation of attributes from stakeholders in chapter 3.

In this case, to get the evaluation started, the director consulted, as stakeholders, the members of the center staff. Their initial discussion of values elicited a list of about 50 verbal descriptors of values. A great many of these were obviously the same idea under a variety of different verbal labels. The director, acting as leader of the discussion, was able to see these duplications and to persuade those who originally proposed these as values to agree on a rephrasing that captured and coalesced these overlapping or duplicating ideas. She did so both because she wanted to keep the list short and because she knew that if the same idea appeared more than once in the final list, she would be "double counting"; that is, including the same value twice. Formally, there is nothing wrong with double counting so long as the *weights* reflect it. But in practice, it is important to avoid, in part

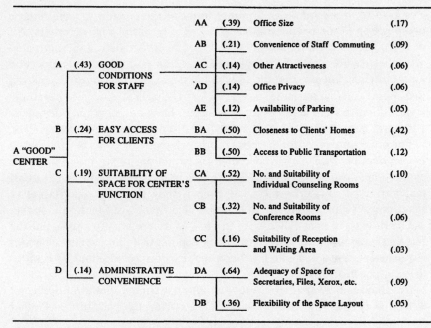

Figure 1: A Value Tree for the Drug-Free Center

because the weights will often not reflect it, and in part because the analysis is typically complex, and addition of extra and unnecessary attributes simply makes the complexity worse.

A second step in editing the list was to eliminate values that, in the view of the stakeholders, could not be important enough to influence the decision. An example of this type of value, considered and then eliminated because it was unimportant, was "proximity to good lunching places." The director was eager to keep the list of values fairly short, and her staff cooperated. In a less collegial situation, elimination of attributes can be much more difficult. Devices that help accomplish it are almost always worthwhile, so long as they do not leave some significant stakeholder feeling that his or her pet values have been summarily ignored.

The director was also able to obtain staff assent to organizing its values into four broad categories, each with subcategories. Such a structure is called a *value tree*. The one that the director worked with is shown in Figure 1. We explain the numbers shortly.

Several questions need review at this stage.

(1) Have all important attributes been listed? Others had been proposed and could obviously have been added. The list does not mention number or location of toilets, proximity to restaurants, presence or absence of other tenants of the same building who might prefer not to have the clients of

this kind of organization as frequent users of the corridors, racial/ethnic composition of the neighborhood, area crime rate, and various others. All of these and many more had been included in earlier lists, and eliminated after discussion. Bases for elimination include not only duplication and unimportance, but also that the sites under consideration did not vary from one another on that attribute, or varied very little. That is why racial/ethnic composition and crime rate were eliminated. Even an important attribute *is* not worth considering unless it contributes to discrimination among sites.

For program evaluation purposes, this principle needs to be considered in conjunction with the purpose of the evaluation. If the function of the evaluation is primarily to guide development of the program, then important attributes should be included even if they serve no discriminative function; in such cases, there may be no discriminative function to serve.

The director was satisfied with the list. It was relatively short, and she felt that it captured the major issues—given the fact that even more major requirements for a new site had been met by prescreening out all options that did not fulfill them.

An obvious omission from the attribute list is cost. For simplicity, we will treat cost as the annual lease cost, ignoring the possibility of other relevant differences among leases.

One possibility would be to treat cost as another attribute, and this is often done, especially for informal or quick evaluations. In such a procedure, one would specify a range of possible costs, assign a weight to that attribute, which essentially amounts to a judgment about how *it* trades off against other attributes, and then include it in the analysis like any other attribute. We have chosen not to do so in this example, for two reasons. First, some evaluations may not involve cost in any significant way (monitoring, for example), and we wish to illustrate procedures for cost independent applications of MAUT. Second, we consider the kind of judgment required to trade off cost against *utility points* to be the least secure and most uncomfortable to make of all those that go into MAUT. For that reason, we like to use procedures, illustrated later, that permit extremely crude versions of that judgment to determine final evaluation.

While on the topic, we should discuss two other aspects of trading off dollars against *aggregated utilities*.

The first is budget constraints. If a budget constrains, in this example, the amount of rent the center can pay, then it is truly a constraint, and sites that fail to meet it must be rejected summarily. More common, however, is the case in which money can be used for one purpose or another. A full analysis would require considering also the loss, in this instance, that would result from spending more on rent and so having less to spend on other things. Such considerations are crucial, but we do not illustrate them here. In order to do so, we would have to provide a scenario about what budget cuts the director would need to make in other categories to pay additional rent. At the time she must choose among sites, she may not know what these are. Fairly often, the expansion of the analysis required to evaluate all possible ways in which a program might be changed by budget reallocations is very large indeed—far too large to make an easy example. So we prefer to think of this as a case in which the director's budget is large enough so that, for the range of costs involved, belt-tightening can take care of the difference between smallest and largest. A fuller analysis would consider the programmatic impact of fund reallocation, and could explore the utility consequences of alternative reallocations. The circumscription of the analysis in the interest of making it manageable is very common; relevant issues are and should be left out of every analysis. (An equivalent statement: If it can be avoided, no MAUT analysis should include every attribute judged relevant by any stakeholder. More on this in chapter 3.) The goal is to enlist stakeholder cooperation in keeping the list of attributes reasonably short.

The other issue having to do with cost but not with the example of this chapter is the portfolio problem. This is the generic name for situations in which a decision maker must choose, not a single option, but a number of options from a larger set. Typically, the limit on the number that can be chosen is specified by a budget constraint. The methods presented in this manual require considerable adaptation to be used formally for portfolio problems, because the decision maker normally wants the portfolio as a whole to have properties such as balance, diversity, or coverage (e.g., of topics, regions, disciplines, problems) that are not attributes of the individual options themselves. Formally, each possible portfolio is an option, and a value tree relevant to the portfolio, not to the individual options, is needed. But such formal complexity is rarely used. A much more common procedure in portfolio problems is to evaluate the individual elements using methods like those of this paper, choose from the best so identified, and then examine the resulting set of choices to make sure that it meets the budget constraint and looks acceptable as a portfolio.

You will have encountered such terms as benefit-cost analysis. Such analyses are similar in spirit to what we are doing here, but quite different in detail. By introducing into the analysis early assumptions about how nonfinancial values trade off with money, both benefits and costs can be expressed in dollar terms. We see little merit in doing so for social programs, since early translation of nonmonetary effects into money terms tends to lead to underassessment of the importance of nonfinancial consequences. The methods we present in this chapter and in chapter 7 are formally equivalent to doing it all in money, but do not require an equation between utility and money until the very end of the analysis, if then. Back to our example. In the initial elicitation of values from the staff, the orderly structure of Figure 1, the value tree, did not appear. Indeed, it took much thought and trial and error to organize the attributes into a tree structure. Formally, only the attributes at the bottom of the tree, which are called *twigs,* are essential for evaluation. Figure 1 is a two-level value tree; that is, all second-level values are twigs. More often, different branches of a value tree will vary in how many levels they have. This paper later presents a four-level example, and examples with as many as fourteen levels exist.

Tree structures are useful in MAUT in three ways. First, they present the attributes in an orderly structure; this helps thought about the problem. Second, the tree structure can make elicitation of importance weights for twigs (which we discuss below) much easier than it would otherwise be, by reducing the number of judgments required. Chapter 4 discusses this further. Finally, value trees permit what we call *subaggregation.* Often a single number is much too compressed a summary of how attractive an option is. Tree structures permit more informative and less compressed summaries. This is further discussed in chapters 6 and 7.

Figure 1 contains a notational scheme we have found useful in value trees. Main branches of the tree are labeled with capital letters, A, B, and so on. Subattributes under each main branch are labeled with double letters, AA, AB, . . . , BA, BB. . . , and so on. This is a two-level tree, so only double letters are needed.

Assignment of Importance Weights

The numbers in Figure 1 are *importance weights* for the attributes. Note that the weights in Figure 1 sum to 1 at each level of the tree. That is, the weights of A, B, C, and D sum to 1. Similarly, the weights of AA through AE sum to 1, as do those of BA and BB and so on. This is a convenient convention, both for elicitation of weights and for their use. The final weights for each attribute at each twig of the tree are easily obtained by "multiplying through the tree." For example, the weight .17 for twig AA (office size) is obtained by multiplying the normalized weight of A (.43) by the normalized weight for AA (.39) to yield $.43 \times .39 = .17$. We discuss multiplying through the tree further in chapter 4.

The weights presented in Figure 1 emerged from a staff meeting in which, after an initial discussion of the idea of weighting, each individual staff member produced a set of weights, using the *ratio method* described in chapter 4. Then all the sets of weights were put on the blackboard, the inevitable individual differences were discussed, and afterward each individual once again used the ratio method to produce a set of weights. These still differed, though by less than did the first set. The final set was produced by averaging the results of the second weighting; the average weights were acceptable to the staff as representing its value system.

The director had some reservations about what the staff had produced, but kept them to herself. She worried about whether the weights associated with staff comfort issues were perhaps too high and those associated with appropriateness to the function of the organization were perhaps too low. (Note that she had no serious reservations about the relative weights within each major branch of the value tree; her concerns were about the relative weights of the four major branches of the tree. This illustrates the usefulness of organizing lists of twigs into a tree structure for weighting.) The director chose to avoid argument with her staff by reserving her concerns about those weights for the sensitivity analysis phase of the evaluation.

Although a common staff set of weights was obtained by averaging (each staff member equally weighted), the individual weights were not thereafter thrown away. Instead, they were kept available for use in the later sensitivity analysis. In general, averaging may be a useful technique if a consensus position is needed, especially for screening options, but it is dangerous, exactly because it obliterates individual differences in weighting. When stakeholders disagree, it is usually a good idea to use the judgments of each separately in evaluation; only if these judgments lead to conflicting conclusions must the sometimes difficult task of reconciling the disagreements be faced. If it is faced, arithmetic is a last resort, if usable at all; discussion and achievement of consensus is much preferred. Often such discussions can be helped by a sensitivity analysis; it will often turn out that the decision is simply insensitive to the weights.

The Assessment of Location Measures or Utilities

With a value tree to guide the choice of measures to take and judgments to make, the next task was to make detailed assessments of each of the six sites that had survived initial screening. Such assessments directly lead to the utilities in multiattribute utility measurement. The word "utility" has a 400-year-old history and conveys a very explicit meaning to contemporary decision analysts. The techniques for obtaining such numbers that we present in this manual deviate in some ways from those implicit in that word. So we prefer to call these numbers *location measures,* since they simply report the location or utility of each object of evaluation on each attribute of evaluation.

Inspect Figure 1 again. Two kinds of values are listed on it. Office size is an objective dimension, measurable in square feet. Office attractiveness is a subjective dimension; it must be obtained by judgment. Proximity to public transportation might be taken in this example as measured by the distance from the front door of the building to the nearest bus stop, which would make it completely objective. But suppose the site were in New York. Then distance to the nearest bus stop and distance to the nearest subway stop would both be relevant and probably the latter would be more important than the former. It would make sense in that case to add another level to the value tree, in which the value "proximity to public transportation" would be further broken down into those two twigs.

As it happens, in Figure 1 all attributes are monotonically increasing; that is, more is better than less. That will not always be true. For some attributes, less is better than more; if "crime rate in the area" had survived the process of elimination that led to Figure 1, it would have been an example. On some attributes, intermediate values are preferable to either extreme; such attributes have a peak inside the range of the attribute. If "racial composition of the neighborhood" had survived as an attribute, the staff might well have felt that the site would score highest on that attribute if its racial/ethnic mix matched that of its clients. If only two racial/ethnic categories were relevant, that would be expressed by a twig, such as "percentage of whites in the neighborhood" that would have a peak at the percentage of whites among the center's clients and would tail off from there in both directions. If more than two racial/ethnic categories were relevant, the value would have been further broken down, with percentage of each relevant racial/ethnic category in the neighborhood as a twig underneath it, and for each of those twigs, the location measure would have a peak at some intermediate value. We will discuss these possibilities and explain how to work with them in chapter 5.

Figure 1 presented the director with a fairly easy assessment task. She chose to make the needed judgments herself. If the problem were more complex and required more expertise, she might well have asked other experts to make some or all of the necessary judgments.

Armed with a tape measure and a notebook, she visited each of the sites, made the relevant measures and counts, and made each of the required judgments. Thus she obtained the raw materials for the location measures.

However, she had to do some transforming on these raw materials. It is necessary for all location measures to be on a common scale, in order for the assessment of weights to make any sense. Although the choice of common scale is obviously arbitrary, we like one in which 0 means horrible and 100 means as well as one could hope to do.

Consider the case of the office size expressed in square feet. It would make no sense to assign the value 0 to 0 sq. ft.; no office could measure 0 sq. ft. After examining her present accommodations and thinking about those of other similar groups, the director decided that an office 60 sq. ft. in size should have a value of 0, and one of 160 sq. ft. should have a value of 100. She also decided that values intermediate between those two limits should be linear in utility. This idea needs explaining. It would be possible to feel that you gain much more in going from 60 to 80 sq. ft. than in going from 140 to 160 sq. ft., and consequently that the scale relating square footage to desirability should be nonlinear. Indeed, traditional utility theory makes that assumption in almost every case.

Curved functions relating physical measurements to utility are probably more precise representations of how people feel than straight ones. But fortunately, such curvature almost never makes any difference to the decision. If it does, the fact that the difference exists means that the options are close enough so that it scarcely matters which is chosen. For that reason, when an appropriate physical scale exists, we advocate choosing maximum and minimum values on it, and then fitting a straight line between those boundaries to translate those measurements into the 0 to 100 scale. We present a fuller discussion of how to do this in chapter 5. Formal arguments in support of our use of linearity are far too technical for this paper; see Edwards (1980) for citations leading to them.

The director did the same kind of thing to all the other attributes for which she had objective measures. The attribute "proximity to clients' homes" presented her with a problem. In principle, she could have chose to measure the linear distance from the address of each current client to each site, average these measures, choose a maximum and minimum value for the average, and then scale each site using the same procedure described for office size. But that would have been much more trouble than it was worth. So instead she looked at a map, drew a circle on it to represent the boundaries of the area that she believed her organization served, and then noted how close each site was to the center of the area. It would have been possible to use radial distance from that center as an objective measure, but she chose not to do so, since clients' homes were not homogeneously distributed within the circle. Instead, she treated this as a directly judgmental attribute, simply using the map as an *aid* to judgment.

Of course, for all judgmental dimensions, the scale is from 0 to 100. For both judgmental and objective attributes, it is important that the scale be realistic. That is, it should be easy to imagine that some of the sites being considered might realistically score 0 to 100 on each attribute.

In this example, since the six sites were known, that could have been assured by assigning a value of 0 to the worst site on a given attribute and a value of 100 to the best on that attribute, locating the others in between. This was not done, and we recommend that it not be done in general. Suppose one of the sites had been rented to someone else, or that a new one turned up. Then if the evaluation scheme were so tightly tied to the specific options available, it would have to be revised. We prefer a procedure in which one attempts to assess realistic boundaries on each relevant attribute with less specific reference to the actual options available. Such a procedure allows the evaluation scheme to remain the same as the option set changes. And the procedure is obviously necessary if the option set is not known, or not fully known, at the time the evaluation scheme is worked out.

It can, of course, happen that a real option turns up that is more extreme than a boundary assigned to some attribute. If that happens, the evaluation scheme can still be used. Two possible approaches exist. Consider, for example, the attribute "access to public transportation" operationalized as distance to the nearest bus stop. One might assign 100 to half a block and 0 to four blocks. Now, suppose two new sites turn up. For one, the bus stop is right in front of the building entrance; for the other, it is five blocks away. The director might well judge that it scarcely matters whether the stop is in front of the building entrance or half a block away, and so assign 100 to all distances of half a block or closer. However, she might also feel that five blocks is meaningfully worse than four. She could handle the five-block case in either of two ways. She might simply disqualify the site on the basis of that fact. Or, if she felt that the site deserved to be evaluated in spite of this disadvantage, she could assign a negative score (it would turn out to be -29; see chapter 5) to that site on that attribute. While such scores outside the 0 to 100 range are not common, and the ranges should be chosen with enough realism to avoid them if possible, nothing in the logic or formal structure of the method prevents their use. It is more important that the range be realistic, so that the options are well spread out over its length, than it is to avoid an occasional instance in which options fall outside it.

Table 4 represents the location measures of the six sites that survived initial screening, transformed onto the 0 to 100 scale. As the director looked at this table, she realized an important point. No matter what the weights, site 6 would never be best in utility. The reason why is that site 2 is at least as attractive as site 6 on all location measures, and definitely better on some. In technical language, site 2 *dominates* site 6. But Table 4 omits one important issue: cost. Checking cost, she found that site 6 was in fact less expensive than site 2, so she kept it in. If it had been as expensive as site 2 or more so, she would have been justified in summarily rejecting it, since it could never beat site 2. No other option dominates or is dominated by another. (Although she might have dropped site 6 if it had not been cheaper than site 2, she would have been unwise to notify the rental office of site 6 that it was out of contention. If for some reason site 2 were to become unavailable, perhaps because it was rented to someone else, then site 6 would once more be a contender.)

Aggregation of Location Measures and Weights

The director now had weights provided by her staff and location measures provided either directly by judgment or by calculations based on measurements. Now her task was to aggregate these into measures of the aggregate utility of each site. The aggregation procedure is the same

TABLE 4

Location Measures for Six Sites

Site Number	AA	AB	AC	AD	AE	BA	BB	CA	CB	CC	DA	DB
							Twig Label					
1	90	50	30	90	10	40	80	10	60	50	10	0
2	50	30	80	30	60	30	70	80	50	40	70	40
3	10	100	70	40	30	0	95	5	10	50	90	50
4	100	80	10	50	100	50	50	50	10	10	50	95
5	20	5	95	10	100	90	5	90	90	95	50	10
6	40	30	80	30	50	30	70	50	50	30	60	40

TABLE 5
Calculation of the Aggregate Utility of Site 1

Twig Label	Weight	Location Measure	Weight × Location Measure
AA	.168	90	15.12
AB	.090	50	4.50
AC	.060	30	1.80
AD	.060	90	5.40
AE	.052	10	0.52
BA	.120	40	4.80
BB	.120	80	9.60
CA	.099	10	.99
CB	.061	60	3.66
CC	.030	50	1.50
DA	.090	10	0.90
DB	.050	0	0.00
SUMS	1.000		48.79

regardless of the depth of the value tree. Simply take the final weight for each twig, multiply it by location measure for that twig, and sum the products. This is illustrated in Table 5 for site 1. In this case, the sum is 48.79, which is the aggregate utility of site 1. It would be possible but tedious to do this for each site. All calculations like that in Table 5 were done with hand calculator programs; the discrepancy between the 48.79 for site 1 of Table 5 and the 48.80 of Table 6 is caused by a rounding process in the program. Table 6 shows the aggregate utilities and the costs for each of the six sites. The costs are given as annual rents.

Now a version of the idea of dominance can be exploited again. In Table 6, the utility values can be considered as measures of desirability and the rents are costs. Obviously, you would not wish to pay more unless you got an increase in desirability. Consequently, options that are inferior to others in both cost and desirability need not be considered further.

On utility, the rank ordering of the sites from best to worst is 425163. On cost, it is 162345. Obviously sites 1 and 4 will be contenders, since 4 is best in utility (with these weights) and 1 is best in cost. Site 5 is dominated, in this aggregated sense, by site 4, and so is out of the race. Sites 3 and 6 are dominated by site 1, and are also out. So sites 1, 2, and 4 remain as *contenders;* 2 is intermediate between 1 and 4 in both utility and cost. This result is general. If a set of options is described by aggregated utilities and costs, and dominated options are removed, than all of the remaining options, if listed in order of increasing utility, will turn out also to be listed in order of increasing cost. This makes the decision problem simpler; it reduces to whether each increment in utility gained from moving from an option lower to one higher in such a list is worth the

TABLE 6
Aggregate Utilities and Rents

Site	Utility	Cost (Rent per year)
1	48.80	$48,000
2	53.26	53,300
3	43.48	54,600
4	57.31	60,600
5	48.92	67,800
6	46.90	53,200

increase in cost. Note that this property does not depend on any numerical properties of the method that will eventually be used to aggregate utility with cost.

A special case arises if two or more options tie in utility, cost, or both. If the tie is in utility, then the one that costs the least among the tied options dominates the others; the others should be eliminated. If they tie in cost, the one with the greatest utility dominates the others; the others should be eliminated. If they tie in both utility and cost, then only one of them need be examined for dominance. If one is dominated, all are; if one is undominated, all are. So either all should be eliminated or all should survive to the next stage of the analysis. Note that a tie in aggregate utility can occur in two different ways: by accident of weighting, or because all location measures are equal. If all location measures are equal, the lower cost will always be preferable to the higher one regardless of weights, so the higher cost can be eliminated not only from the main analysis, but from all sensitivity analyses. If they tie in aggregate utility by accident of weighting, changes in weight will ordinarily untie them, and so the tied options must be included in the sensitivity analysis.

If the option that represents the tie emerges from the next stage of the analysis looking best, the only way to discriminate it from its twins is by sensitivity analysis, by considering other attributes, or both.

Nothing guarantees that the dominance analysis we just performed will eliminate options. If the ordering in utility had been 123456 and the ordering in cost had been 654321 (just the opposite) no option would have dominated any other, and none could have been eliminated. Such perfect relationships between cost and utility are rare, except perhaps in the marketplace, in which dominated options may be eliminated by market pressure.

The decision about whether to accept an increase in cost in order to obtain an increase in utility is often made intuitively, and that may be an excellent way to make it. But arithmetic can help. In this example, consider Table 7. It lists the three contending sites, 1, 2, and 4, in order of increasing

TABLE 7
Incremental Utilities and Costs for the Siting Example

Site No.	Utility Differences (Increment)	Cost Differences (Increment)	Cost Incr./ Utility Incr.
1	0	0	
2	4.46	$5300	$1188
4	4.05	$7300	$1802

utility and cost. In the second column, each entry is the utility of that site minus the utility of the site just above it. Thus, for example, the 4.05 utility difference associated with site 4 is obtained by subtracting the aggregate utility of 2 from that of 4 in Table 6: 57.31–53.26 = 4.05. Similarly, the cost difference of $7,300 for site 4 is obtained from Table 6 in the same way: $60,600–53,300 = $7,300. The other numbers in the second and third columns are calculated similarly. The fourth column is simply the number in the third column divided by the number in the second.

The numbers in the fourth column increase from top to bottom. This means that all three sites are true contenders. This is not necessarily the case. In chapter 7, we present what happens and what to do if that column does not increase continuously as in Table 7.

The last column of Table 7 also serves another purpose. Since it is the increase in cost divided by the increase in utility, it is a dollar value for one utility point. Specifically, it is the dollar value for one utility point that would be just enough to cause you to prefer the higher cost site to the lower cost one. If the dollar value of a utility point is less than $1,188, you should choose site 1; if it is between $1,188 and $1,802, you should choose site 2; and if it is above $1,802, you should choose site 4.

But how can you know the dollar value of a utility point, for yourself or for other stakeholders? The judgment obviously need not be made with much precision—but it is, if formulated in that language, an impossible judgment to make. But it need not be formulated in that language. Consider instead the following procedure. Refer back to Figure 1. First pick a twig that you have firm and definite opinions about. Suppose it is DA, availability and suitability of space for secretaries, files, Xerox, and the like. Now, ask of yourself and of the other stakeholders, "How much money would it be worth to improve that twig by so many points?" The typical number of points to use in such questions is 100, so the question becomes: "How much would it be worth to improve the availability and suitability of space for secretaries, files, Xerox, and the like from the minimum acceptable state, to which I have assigned a location measure of 0, to a state to which I would assign a location measure of 100?"

TABLE 8
Aggregate Utilities after Subtracting Penalties for Excess Cost

Site No.	Value of a 100 point swing in DA (weight = .09)		
	S9,000	$13,500	$18,000
1	48.80	48.80	48.80
2	47.96	49.73	50.61
4	44.71	48.91	51.01

Such a question, asked of various stakeholders, will elicit various answers; a compromise or agreed-on number should be found. Suppose, in this example, that it turned out to be $13,500. Now, refer to Table 5 and note that the twig weight for DA is .090. Consequently, a 100-point change in DA will change aggregate utility by $100 \times .090 = 9$ points—for this particular set of weights. Note, incidentally, that while, the 9-point number depends on the weights, the judgment of the dollar value of a 100-point change in DA does not. Consequently, if you choose to change weights (as we will in chapter 7 on sensitivity analysis), you will need to recalculate the value of a utility point, but will not need to obtain a new dollar value judgment of this kind from anyone.

If a 9-point change in utility is worth $13,500, then a 1-point change in utility is worth $13,500/9 = $1,500$. So, using the weights on which this chapter is based, site 2 is clearly preferable to sites 1 and 4 since $1,500 is between $1,188 and $1,802.

Let us verify that statement. One way to do so is to penalize the more expensive sites by a number of utility points appropriate for their increase in cost. Thus, if utility is worth $1,500 per point, and site 2 costs $5,300 more than site 1, then site 2 should be penalized $5,300 / 1,500 = 3.53$ utility points in order to make it comparable to site 1. Similarly, if utility is worth $1,500 per point, then site 4 should be penalized by the increment in its costs over site 1, $5,300 + $7,300 = $12,600, divided by the dollar value of a point; $12,600 / 1,500 = 8.40$ utility points. This makes all three sites comparable; by correcting each of the more expensive ones by the utility equivalent of the additional expense. So now the choice could be based on utility alone.

Table 8 makes the same calculation for all three sites and for three different judgments of how much a 9-point swing in aggregate utility is worth: $9,000, $13,500, and $18,000; these correspond, with the weights used in this chapter, to utility values per point of $1,000, $1,500, and $2,000, respectively. Table 8 is included here not because it is a calculation that the director would ever need to make, but because it demonstrates that the choices made on the basis of Table 7, which is a calculation she might well need to make, are appropriate.

As illustrated in Table 8, a utility value of $1,000 per point makes site 1 best, a utility value of $1,500 per point makes site 2 best, and a utility value of $2,000 per point makes site 4 best. Note, however, that the differences in corrected utilities are relatively small. This is normal, and is one reason why we make no strong case for using such calculations to go from Table 6 to Table 8. Elimination of noncontenders is usually both more important and easier to do than selection among those that survive the elimination process, since the survivors are likely to be close enough to one another in attractiveness so that no choice will be disastrous.

Sensitivity Analysis

The director of the center had some doubt about the weights her staff had given her. She therefore considered various other weights. We present the details in chapter 7 on sensitivity analysis. She found a set of weights that make site 5 best in utility, and another for which site 2 is best.

Chapter 7 also presents a minor example of exploring sensitivity to location measures. But the director was relatively well satisfied with the location measures she was using, and felt no need to change them—and she also felt that there were so many that she was unsure which ones to change.

At this point the director felt she had enough information and analysis to make her recommendation of site 2. Details of how the sensitivity analysis convinced her that site 2 was best are presented in chapter 7.

Summary

Chapter 2 presents an example in detail. A social service center needs to move; six sites are available. Using staff weights applied to a value tree with twelve twigs, the director of the center is able to eliminate three of the six sites and to reach a conclusion among the other three.

Various technical problems arise and are discussed in presentation of the example. One is cost. The analysis treats cost as an evaluative attribute but keeps it separate from all other attributes until the end. Dominance techniques are used to eliminate options based on aggregated utilities and cost. An illustration is given of how judgments or trade-offs between cost and all other attributes can be used as a basis for a single multiattributed evaluation of what option is best. A second problem is how the nature of the context affects detailed definitions of values. A third is how to deal with options that fall outside anticipated ranges on one or more values. A fourth is how to go about operationalizing some values in order to obtain location measures. The last is what to do about ties in value, cost, or both.

3. THE SOURCE OF VALUE ATTRIBUTES: THE CONCEPT OF STAKEHOLDERS AND THE STRUCTURE OF VALUES[2]

The approach to evaluation, Multiattribute Utility Technology (MAUT), advocated in this paper relies heavily on the measurement of utility (subjective value of the entity or project being evaluated). But values tend to be personal and therefore are usually associated with individuals or groups. The generic name for such individuals and/or groups is *stakeholders,* people who have an interest or a stake in the program or the entity being evaluated, and who are important enough so that their interests should be considered. Stakeholders are often at the policy level of decision making, concerned with the program goals and objectives and the consequences of program operations. The main tasks performed by the stakeholders in evaluation are to identify and structure the value attributes important to the evaluation, and to assign importance weights to these attributes, the topic discussed in chapter 4.

In the site location example, the stakeholder may be a single individual, the director of the drug counseling center, or it may be a group or committee charged with the responsibility of relocating to a new site such as staff members of the center. Other stakeholders include the sponsor, the court, the probation department, and the center's clients.

In this chapter we concentrate on the problem of identifying the stake holders and eliciting the value attributes from them. We also illustrate how these attributes might be structured or organized.

Who Are the Stakeholders?

We distinguish between *actors*—people who may make decisions about the program and perhaps take direct action to change it, and those people who are affected or impinged upon by the program, either directly or indirectly. Both of these types of stakeholders should be involved in an evaluation, although their roles are different. The actors make the decisions to which the evaluation should be relevant. Therefore, they can best explicate what values should be considered in their decisions.

People who are affected by a program have a different role. Their values enter less directly—but not necessarily less importantly—into decisions. Among the values relevant to decisions (presumably *high* among them for many decisions) is how the program affects people. Thus, the evaluation can enhance programmatic decisions by explicitly and accurately representing the values of these affected people.

Virtually all social programs will have many stakeholders. The primary actors are usually the most easily identified. Begin by examining the organizational structure of the program. If the program has multiple local projects, are these projects homogeneous enough to be considered as involving a single set of stakeholders, or is the program an "umbrella" under which are varied projects whose decision makers will have different values and objectives? Single local projects may, in fact, have two sets of decision makers: those responsible for managing the project, and those responsible for the general administration of the organizations conducting the project.

In rare instances, the program being evaluated will be a unitary program with a single level of decision-making authority. In the more common case, the next level up in the decision-making hierarchy depends on the type of program being evaluated. For umbrella-type programs, it may be the program office in the nongovernmental or governmental agency administering the program. For other programs, it may be a local agency, either governmental or private.

If the local programs are funded with block grant money, the State Planning Agency (SPA) that administers the block grants may also be a relevant stakeholder. Within the federal sponsoring agency, there may be stakeholders in addition to the program office. The administration may be a stakeholder, and the office funding the evaluation (not necessarily the same as the program office) may be a stakeholder. Then, of course, there is the relevant legislature, one of the ultimate organizational decision makers, which will probably need to be considered a stakeholder if the program has been legislatively mandated.

The above discussion does not fit all social programs. It is intended only to illustrate how an evaluator might begin to identify just who the relevant decision makers are. Stakeholders who are not decision makers, but rather are people or organizations affected by the program, may be more difficult to identify. The clients of the program are such stakeholders, as are other members of the target population who for one reason or another are not actual clients. If the target population does not coincide with the population of the target area, the remainder of the target area population may be affected by the program. Juvenile programs would create this category of stakeholder, such as parents and teachers of the juvenile offenders.

Beyond these populations and agencies, stakeholders may include special interest groups that have a particular concern with the program being evaluated. The nature of these groups would depend on the type of program being evaluated.

Most evaluations will have neither the resources nor the need to work closely with all identified potential stakeholders. Enough interaction with the less significant stakeholders is necessary to ensure their representation in the evaluation. However, any stakeholder likely to use evaluation in making decisions requires careful attention from and extensive interaction with the evaluation staff. Such stakeholders need to feel that the evaluation, or at least a particular part of the evaluation, is being done for them—and it should be. Identifying such decisions and the stakeholders who make them may easily tax the knowledge and political skills of evaluators up to or beyond their limits.

Identification of stakeholders will depend in part, obviously, on the purpose of the evaluation. Stakeholders for an evaluation of the feasibility of a program before it is installed will include the legislators or others, typically public officials, who are responsible for the fact that the program is under consideration. They will also include speakers for the organization who may be influenced by the new program if it is implemented. If at least some program staff are already selected, they are stakeholders. In this as in all other programs, stakeholders include representatives of the public interest and of the clients whom the program may affect.

Essentially the same list of stakeholders applies to evaluations being conducted during the early stages of a program to see if it is on track—sometimes called formative evaluations. However, the emphasis is some what different. Program people and those directly impacted by the program are especially important in this kind of evaluation. The same is true for monitoring. In both of these cases, too, the sponsor(s) are important.

The most traditional idea of evaluation is that it is concerned with measuring the external impact of a program—finding out whether or not it is fulfilling its goals. For such an evaluation, the list of stakeholders is much the same, but the emphasis changes. In evaluating the consequences of a program, stakeholders from outside the program have much more importance than is the case for monitoring. In some such cases, it is useful to treat independent academics and others as though they were stakeholders, as is the case in use of review panels. Those external to the program who are affected by it, including agencies of various kinds, representatives of public interests, and representatives of client interests, are especially important. If the program is a topic of debate, obviously the sides to that debate are stakeholders.

Although everyone wants to have his or her finger in public pies, the implication of the preceding paragraphs is that evaluations intended basically to guide the internal workings of a program need less heavy involvement of outside stakeholders than evaluations intended to guide major programmatic decisions. But the other implication is that, to whatever limits money, time, and cooperativeness make necessary, it is always better to include too many stakeholders than too few. Normally, the evaluator will be in conflict; well aware of omissions from the list of participating stakeholders, he or she will still find that list inconveniently long. As usual, difficult choices must be made.

Eliciting Value Structures from Stakeholders

Involvement, and getting people to pay attention to results (regardless of whether they agree or disagree with them), are enhanced by communicating with both critical actors and representatives of affected groups at the outset of the evaluation. It is crucial to determine what types of decisions may be made, and to consider at least crudely what factors may critically affect them. Political issues of concern to legislators, for example, are of at best indirect concern to project managers and clients. The first step, therefore, is to query groups and individuals about what values *from their perspective* the program may affect.

One should perhaps begin with staff (administrators and managers) and clients of the program, but should also ensure that critical actors (e.g., legislative figures) with a view of the topic are queried. One advantage of beginning with staff and clients is that the evaluator needs detailed knowledge about the program, and this is a good source. The elicitation of relevant values can begin with statements about the objectives of the program, e.g., reduce crime or reduce recidivism for criminal justice programs. Presumably, the program is expected to produce a change on these value attributes. But care must be taken not to consider only the programmatic objectives. Other values may also be affected by the program, so care must be taken to discuss possible "spin-off" effects with stakeholders. This is particularly true of value attributes that the program may affect negatively, since stakeholders, especially if interviewed early, may be predominantly supporters of the program.

One pattern that we have observed is that legislators will express objectives about performance by the agency implementing the program, the agency will have objectives both about its performance and about the performance of individual projects funded through the program, and the individual projects will have their own objectives. More generally, everyone seems to have objectives for that part of the program for which they are immediately responsible. Given the complex administrative and management arrangements of typical programs, this implies several sets of values than can be expected to coincide to some degree but certainly not completely.

We illustrate this by the evaluation of the Community Anti-Crime (CAC) program administered by the Office of Community Anti-Crime Programs (OCAP) within the Law Enforcement Assistance Administration (LEAA). As implemented, its basic idea was that local community organizations interested in adopting some mix of strategies for reducing the incidence of crime could apply for money to LEAA's OCAP. One goal of the program, a goal encouraged by Congress, was to reduce red tape. Consequently, grants went directly from LEAA to the applying organization—which might not even have been sufficiently highly structured to meet normal federal standards of stability and of capability for financial accounting. Another goal, also encouraged by congressional supporters, was to encourage the invention of innovative anticrime strategies. This goal, in turn, gave OCAP every reason to seek a wide variety of different activities among its grantees. Moreover, since another program objective was community involvement, any simple measure such as crime statistics for the relevant communities would miss a major point of the program. Also, the National Institute for Law Enforcement and Criminal Justice (NILECJ) was a distinct unit from OCAP within LEAA; it was concerned with research questions and the evaluation process itself. The expressed concerns of Congress, OCAP, NILECJ, and any Community Work Group involved with crime prevention necessarily reflected their differences in perspective concerning what an anticrime program was all about, but these were not necessarily inconsistent for developing the evaluation from the viewpoint of a MAUT model. The problem was a practical one of culling out, from each group, those objectives that were in fact relevant to the intended purpose of the evaluation model. If the purpose is to assess program effectiveness, only values related directly to the effects of the program should be included. Unless the various organizational entities are working at explicit cross-purposes, it should be possible to structure the values into a single, internally consistent MAUT model. Also, it will often be possible to develop a MAUT model structure that more or less parallels organizational structures themselves. We have two specific recommendations about how to do this.

(1) Separate value attributes from topics people are merely curious about. If one is not careful, asking stakeholders for attributes will yield a hodgepodge of topics. Included will be topics the respondent is curious about but that are clearly not value attributes ("it would be nice to know what kind of communities are especially likely to get involved in this type of program"), as well as topics that seem plausible candidates for value attributes but on reflection are not appropriate ("we want to make better decisions about which applicants to fund in the future"). In this latter case, the quality of future decisions about applicants has no bearing on how the effectiveness of current projects themselves should be assessed.

Two kinds of extraneous topics are likely to arise as pseudo-attributes. The first, often of interest to researchers, is information one would like to have about the program or related social phenomena that is really quite irrelevant to assessing the utility or value of the program itself. The second has to do with the utilization of the evaluation itself. People want to disseminate evaluation results, either to make better decisions or in order to argue some case before the decisions are made. So they want to determine what data (and in what form) the evaluation should feed into the decision process. Elsewhere we discuss in more detail the dynamic nature of program policy making, planning, and management; but at the present it is sufficient to note that programmatic monitoring (and relatively informal decisions about whether the program is doing "well" or not) typically will rely much more heavily on the programmatic data than will many fundamental policy decisions. Policy decisions, for example, will typically involve comparisons among other programs that are competing for money or other support, and often get tied up in political processes and negotiations. The actors may not have articulated for themselves what decisions may be made, and the task of probing them may (and often will) fall to the evaluator.

To help ferret out legitimate programmatic objectives from extraneous topics, it is useful to ask repeatedly whether a given attribute actually relates to the value of the program; if the attribute varies, so will one's opinion about the value of the program. Another useful device is to list some relevant measures or statistics pertaining to the "value attributes," and to ask whether these are valid indicators of programmatic value. Often, consideration of specific statistics (i.e., operationalization of the value attribute) will help sharpen perceptions about what a given value attribute actually means. It is useful for the evaluators to reflect for a while on the lists of candidate value attributes to attempt to identify extraneous items. And of course, the final check is always to go back to the stakeholders with some specific questions about which items should or should not be counted as true value attributes for the program. This often helps to make previously unstated values explicit.

(2) Standardize terminology: Eliminate "distinctions without a difference." Essentially the same value attribute can be stated in many ways. When querying stakeholders, standardizing terminology is useful, and most commonly held value attributes can be identified in this manner. Sometimes, however, it is useful to consider specific measures or statistics, and to ask whether these in fact seem to reflect fundamentally different value attributes. That is, one wishes to avoid "distinctions without a difference."

It is very important to clarify definitions before an attempt is made to structure the value attributes into a MAUT model. Otherwise, the model is likely to include some value attributes that produce the severest form of double-counting: They are just plain redundant.

Structuring the MAUT Model

Models should involve a decomposition of overall program value into its component attributes. Earlier we suggested that there may be a tendency for stakeholders to articulate objectives pertaining to that aspect of the program with which they are most directly involved. This has two impli-

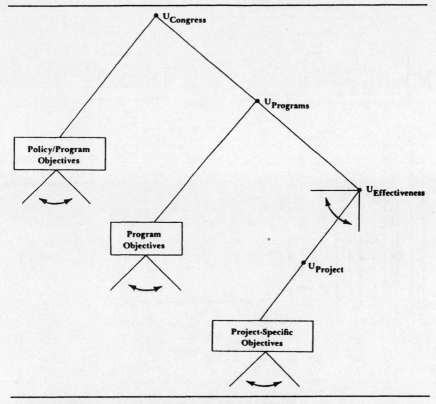

Figure 2: The Clusters of Objectives (Value Attributes) for CAC

cations. First, each group will give only part of the total set of value attributes, and one must amalgamate across stakeholders to get the whole. Second, the structure of the MAUT model itself will often parallel the organizational relationships among the stakeholder groups. Specifically, it will often be possible to organize the MAUT model so that different clusters of value attributes may be more or less imputed to identifiable groups.

This situation is shown in Figure 2 for the CAC program. For this evaluation the value attributes were formulated as "objectives." "Policy/program objectives" are those Congress had for the program, whereas "program objectives" are those the program office set both for itself and for constituent projects funded under the program. Finally, "project specific objectives" were those the local projects set for themselves. This general model, in fact, described accurately the MAUT model developed for the CAC evaluation (see Figure 3). In Figure 3, the Office of Community Anti-Crime Programs (OCAP) was the program office, and it had

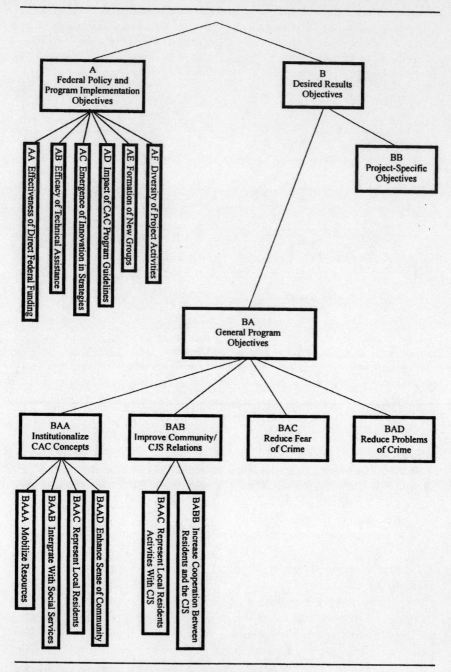

Figure 3: The Hierarchy of CAC Objectives (Value Attributes)

"results sought" objectives in two main areas. Similarly, there were program/ policy objectives specified by congressional staff. Figure 3 does not show them, but submodels would have to be developed for various specific projects. These would be represented by further branching under "project-specific objectives" (BB).

Multiple Stakeholders and a Common Value Tree

Nothing guarantees that the values elicited from different stakeholders will be similar enough so that they can all be arrayed in the same value tree. Indeed, attempting to do just that is one of the most demanding tasks that a user of MAUT may have to face.

So far, we have not encountered any instances in which, with enough hard thought and time to discuss the matter with stakeholders, this could not be done. It is obviously extremely useful to do it. While different stakeholders using different value tree structures can perform or have performed for them the same MAUT evaluation of the same entities, there is no obvious way of relating one evaluation to another unless the tree structures are the same. If the tree structures are the same, the differences among stakeholders can be described as differences in weights and perhaps also in preferred location measures. Differences in preferred location measures can also be described as differences in weights, since various different measures that purport to measure the same kind of value can be considered as simply another level of the value tree. We consider conflicts about weights to be easier both to interpret and to discuss and, perhaps, to resolve than conflicts about structure, mostly because they lend themselves so easily to compromises. Some unpublished experience backs this up.

Among the devices that an imaginative evaluator can use to make one larger value tree out of those elicited from several stakeholders, the most obvious (requiring, however, cooperation from the stakeholders) is combining categories from different stakeholders by relabeling or otherwise recognizing intellectual similarity behind verbal difference. Another method helpful in persuading a stakeholder to include values that seem unimportant is to make the point that that stakeholder can make any value utterly unimportant simply by assigning it zero weight. Still another, illustrated in the CAC example, is to include the values of stakeholders at various levels of an organizational hierarchy, by making the hierarchical structure of the value tree correspond more or less to that of the organization. Indeed, so blunt a device as simply listing values of different stakeholders as different branches of a value tree is always available as a last resort. This paper will hereafter assume that the evaluator, though working with different weights from different stakeholders, has managed to boil the values down to a common value tree.

Identification of Measures in a MAUT Model

When value attributes are formulated as program objectives as in the CAC program, a logical next step would be to identify measures of how well these objectives have been obtained. While this is primarily the topic for a later chapter (chapter 5), it might help clarification if we illustrated this in the context of the CAC evaluation. In program evaluation, attainment of some objectives must be assessed wholly judgmentally. That is, experts will make direct ratings about how fully objectives are attained. We will confine ourselves here to the usual case, in which there are data that can be used to assess actual degree of attainment.

To illustrate, Table 9 shows measures that were identified as relevant to the objectives shown in Figure 3. Two or three measures are shown for each objective, selected from lists that are typically much larger.

In deciding which specific measures (from a list of several alternatives) should be actually included in the model, there is little premium for choosing and including large numbers of measures. Rather, the emphasis should be on including those thought to be most reliable and valid. Variables of marginal relevance or suspect validity should generally not be included. This advice is inappropriate, of course, if such measures are the best available for some important twig of the value tree.

A Comment About Different Measures

Often, there will be multiple, imperfect measures of a given objective; alternative measures may, in fact, be proposed as relevant by different stakeholders. Sometimes, especially in an area of hot political debate, the disagreements about appropriate measures may be severe. This is most likely to happen if disagreeing stakeholders are committed to different answers to a policy question, and therefore want to use measures that will make a particular answer look good or bad. A case in point is the evaluation of nuclear power plants. An obvious value relevant to evaluation of such a plant, either prospectively or retrospectively, is accidents. Subdivisions under that value might be number and severity. But subdivisions under each of those headings could easily be topics of intense debate. Is a malfunction that causes the emergency mechanisms of the reactor to shut it down an accident, or an event incidental to normal operation? If a malfunction occurs and the emergency mechanisms fail to work, but alert response by the reactor crew shuts the reactor down without damage or release of radioactive materials, is that an accident? Suppose the same scenario occurs, but some damage to the core occurs and some radioactive materials are released within the pressure container, but not beyond it? Similarly, consider measures of severity of an accident that does release radioactive materials beyond the pressure container.

Expected number of fatalities is a familiar measure for industrial accidents. A more common one in the nuclear reactor field, however, is expected fatalities from the maximum credible accident.

We do not offer any suggestions about how to resolve such disputes other than the obvious one that whenever more than one measure of the same value is proposed, it seems natural to treat these as complementary to one another, rather than competitive, and therefore to use all. Then the problem becomes one of weighting them for aggregation, rather than of deciding which to include and which to exclude. We have seen little evidence that this suggestion, which seems very practical to us, is likely to be used in the nuclear debate. Pro-nuclear advocates want measures that make nuclear plants look safe; antinuclear advocates want measures that make nuclear plants look dangerous. The techniques described in this paper are unlikely to help in such polarized, institutionalized conflicts. They are better suited to more open-minded stakeholders. Fortunately, our experience in using MAUT in both types of conflicts suggests that participants in the nuclear power controversy occupy positions with uniquely extreme intransigence; even conflicts about forced school busing are milder.

Two Other Examples

We present two more examples of stakeholders and the origin of the value attributes. One is from the area of civil justice, and the other from educational policy implementation. Both were designed by the Social Science Research Institute (SSRI) of the University of Southern California (USC).

**EXAMPLE: THE EVALUATION OF
THE OFFICE OF THE RENTALSMAN**

The Province of British Columbia, Canada, is experimenting with an interesting alternative to the courts in resolving disputes between landlords and tenants: the Office of the Rentalsman (OR). As a dispute resolution mechanism, the OR was unusual in its inception and operation in the sense that it was set up as a distinct alternative to the court and operated completely separate from the court. The legislation that created the OR removed jurisdiction of landlord/tenant disputes involving residential property (commercial property was excluded from the act) from the court and gave it exclusively to the OR. The OR operates quite differently from the court in resolving landlord/tenant disputes. It provides an extensive information service, including a toll-free answering service that landlords and tenants can call and ask questions about what their rights and limitations are. The court provided no such function. A dispute can be brought

TABLE 9

Measures of the CAC Objectives (value attributes)

AA *Effectiveness of Direct Federal Funding Strategy*
- Number of organizations receiving specific CAC funding. (This means that the organizations receive a specific amount of money which they effectively control.)
- Average percentage of grant funds spent on administration.
- Average percent of grant funds spent on equipment.

AB *Efficacy of Technical Assistance to CAC Projects*
- Percentage of projects receiving TA prior to grant award.
- Percentage of projects satisfied with the TA they received.
- Ratings of TA by evaluation staff as part of Levels II and III Observer Reports.

AC *Emergence of Innovation in Project Strategies*
- Percentage of projects with innovative activities.
- Percentage of projects that do not just continue or expand previous activities.
- Percentage of projects with activities not specified in AIR MIS.

AD *Impact of CAC Program Guidelines on Projects*
- Percentage of activities not suggested in the Guidelines.
- Ratings by projects of usefulness and restrictiveness of the Guidelines.

BAAD *Enhance Sense of Community*
- Percentage of residents who think there has been an increase in the past year in people in the neighborhood helping each other.
- Percentage of residents who have increased the number of neighborhood residents with whom they are acquainted in the past year.
- Percentage of residents who have joined a block club or neighborhood organization in the past year.
- Ratings of neighborhood improvement by evaluation staff on Observer Reports.

BABA *Coordinate Anti-Crime Activities with CJS*
- Percentage of projects establishing a link with the police.
- Percentage of projects with an *active* role for the police.
- Percentage of projects with activities (other than above) directly involving the CJS.

BABB *Improve Resident Attitudes Toward the Police*
- Percentage of residents who think police respond faster to calls than they did a year ago.
- Percentage of residents who think police/community relations have improved in the past year.
- Percentage of residents who think police treatment of residents has improved in the past year.

AE

Formation of New Groups
- Number of new coalitions formed to receive grants.
- Number of new organizations formed.
- Average time in existence for new organizations.
- Average number of members of new organizations.

AF

Diversity of Project Activities
- Percentage of projects with components for youth.
- Percentage of projects with components for the elderly.
- Percentage of projects conducting activities addressing both "causal factors" and "opportunity reduction."

BAAB

Institutionalize Project Activities: Integrate with Other Social Services
- Percentage of projects being run by organizations that also provide other services.
- Percentage of projects exchanging referrals with organizations providing other social services.
- Ratings in evaluation staff Observer Reports of relationships with other community organizations.

BAAC

Represent Local Residents
- Percentage of projects with resident involvement in policy decision-making.
- Percentage of projects with resident involvement in budget decision-making.
- Percentage of projects with resident involvement in staff selection.

BAC

Reduce Fear of Crime
- Percentage of residents who now feel safer out alone in the neighborhood during the day than they did a year ago.
- Percentage of residents who are now less often worried about personal attacks during the daytime than they were a year ago.

BAD

Reduce Problem of Crime and Victimization
- Percentage of residents who think the severity of robbery as a problem in the neighborhood has been reduced in the past year.
- Percentage of residents who think the severity of stranger assault as a problem in the neighborhood has been reduced in the past year.
- Percentage of residents who think the severity of burglary as a problem in the neighborhood has been reduced in the past year.

BB

Project Specific Objectives
- Local projects can be expected to have objectives of their own that do not coincide exactly with the general program objectives. Since this Program recognizes the diversity in various communities, attainment of these project-specific objectives that reflect this diversity is desirable. Of course, no general statement of these objectives can be presented. Rather, some individual projects are being selected and their specific objectives will be delineated and evaluated in an appropriate manner.
- The objectives and measures for selected projects enter into the overall model as submodels, branching under "Project-specific objectives" in Exhibit 3.

45

to the OR in many ways such as by a telephone call, via the mail, or just by walking into an OR office and filing a complaint. The court, on the other hand, had only one mechanism for filing a complaint. A great deal of mediation goes on in the OR, whereas the court only adjudicated. If a case is serious enough, a hearing is held by an OR officer, and these hearings are similar to court hearings, although considerably less formal.

The Stakeholders and the Attributes. The evaluation of the OR was concerned not only with measuring how effective the OR was or might be in doing its job, but also with obtaining some information about how it compared with the previous mechanism for resolving landlord/tenant disputes, namely the court. Thus the identification of the stakeholders consisted of seeking out those persons who were knowledgeable about both the current operation of the OR and the court procedure for dispute resolution. Among the stakeholders selected were judges, representatives of landlord and tenant organizations, legal scholars concerned with landlord/tenant issues, and, of course, OR staff members. Each person was individually asked to list his or her attributes of importance for the operation of the OR. The attributes, 16 in all, that finally emerged from this process along with their respective definitions are listed in Figure 4. It should be noted, and this is typical, that there is considerable "overlap" in the attributes. For example, the attributes of *fairness* and *impartiality* might be considered the same thing, although there are subtle differences in these two attri- butes that, in this study at any rate, the experts wished to retain. The attributes given in Figure 4 can be placed in a value tree and this is done in Figure 5.

There is another point to be noted in Figures 4 and 5. Two attributes listed by the stakeholders, *cost* (to the users) and *expense* (to the institution or taxpayer), are not always considered attributes of importance. As mentioned in chapter 2, cost considerations often do not enter until presentation of the final results. In this particular evaluation, making direct statements about cost of services in terms of dollars was not possible. Almost all of the stakeholders, however, included either *cost* or *expense* in their list of attributes. Thus they were retained in the evaluation as attributes.

The listing of attributes and the specification of a value tree can get quite complicated as the next example will illustrate.

EXAMPLE: THE EVALUATION OF SCHOOL DESEGREGATION PLANS IN LOS ANGELES

As with other school districts across the nation the Los Angeles Unified School District (LAUSD) was recently forced by a court order to desegregate its schools. Several desegregation/integration plans had been prepared

Accessibility—ease of registering requests and complaints; taking into consideration procedural complexity, hours/days available, and physical location.

Consistency—the degree to which the institution's decisions reflect general rules.

Cost—cost in dollars or dollar-equivalents (e.g., time) for the individuals to secure the services of the institution.

Education—the degree to which the institution provides information to members of the public about their rights, obligations, and remedies to disputes.

Expense—cost to the institution for providing the services which it provides.

Expertise—the degree to which the institution is familiar with the types of disputes and questions generally submitted to it.

Fairness—the extent to which the process reflects natural justice and general equity.

Flexibility—the degree to which the institution's decisions reflect general rules of the circumstances of the particular parties involved in disputes.

Impartiality—the extent to which decisions do *not* give special consideration to either landlords or tenants or to any irrelevant attributes of any disputants.

Independence/Accountability—the degree and consistency with which the institution's behavior is directly influenced by other institutions (e.g., electorate, ministry, private associations, public opinion).

Informality—the degree to which the dispute process does not follow a prescribed pattern.

Investigative Power—the extent to which the institution takes responsibility for investigating facts.

Jurisdiction—the degree to which jurisdictional limitations on the institution's operations are a problem for the parties involved in disputes.

Power—the ease with which the institution can enforce the orders which it issues.

Speed—the length of time the institution takes to provide information and process disputes.

Visibility—the extent to which citizens are aware of the Office and its functions.

Figure 4: The Value Attributes as Identified by the Experts for the Office of the Rentalsman (listed alphabetically)

A Resolution Process	B Action Process	C Administrative Process	D Financial Process
AA Fairness	BA Power (to enforce decisions)	CA Accessibility	DA Cost (to individual)
AB Impartiality	BB Investigative Power	CB Education	DB Expense (to the institution)
AC Expertise	BC Independence/Accountability	CC Visibility	
AD Flexibility		CD Speed	
AE Consistency			
AF Jurisdiction			
AG Informality			

Figure 5: Value Tree: Office of the Rentalsman

and submitted to the Los Angeles School Board. A method of evaluating these was needed and a MAUT evaluation was carried out for this purpose.

The Stakeholders and the Attributes. In this case the major stakeholders were the members of the Los Angeles School Board. Since they were elected officials, in principle these board members represented the "ultimate stakeholders: the citizens of Los Angeles City concerned with public education." However, a preliminary listing of the attributes was done by the evaluator (Dr. Ward Edwards of USC) working closely with several members of the LAUSD staff. Several versions were prepared and presented to members of the Board of Education and to representatives of pro and con desegregation groups and other interveners. Comments from these groups were elicited; value attributes were changed, added, dropped (mostly added). The eighth and final version of the value tree is presented in Figure 6. This was such a complex tree that there is no way to combine the elements and the structure in a single-page display. Consequently, Figure 6 shows the structure only. The letters inside Figure 6 refer to the particular value attributes included in the tree broken down from the most general to the most specific. The major attributes are:

(A)   Effect of a desegregation plan on racial/ethnic compositions.
(B)   Effect of a desegregation plan on educational quality.
(C)   Community acceptance of a desegregation plan.
(D)   Implications of a desegregation plan for district personnel.
(E)   Destabilizing effects of a desegregation plan.
(F)   Provisions within a desegregation plan for monitoring and evaluation.

Under A of Figure 6 we have:

(AA)   Racial/ethnic proportions of pupils moved from local schools.
(AB)   Racial/ethnic proportions in resulting schools.
(AC)   Racial/ethnic proportions of pupils bused. (Note: originally we expected some nonbusing plans. None were submitted, so this branch was treated like AA.)
(AD)   Number of grades affected by reassignments.
(AE)   Duration in weeks of integrated educational experience.
(AF)   Numbers of students remaining in isolated schools.
(AG)   Provisions for reduction of racial/ethnic isolation in still segregated schools.
(AH)   Provisions for effectively preventing the resegregation of integrated schools.

The remaining subattributes of A and the major attributes B, C, and so on of Figure 6 were detailed out in a manner similar to A and will not be presented

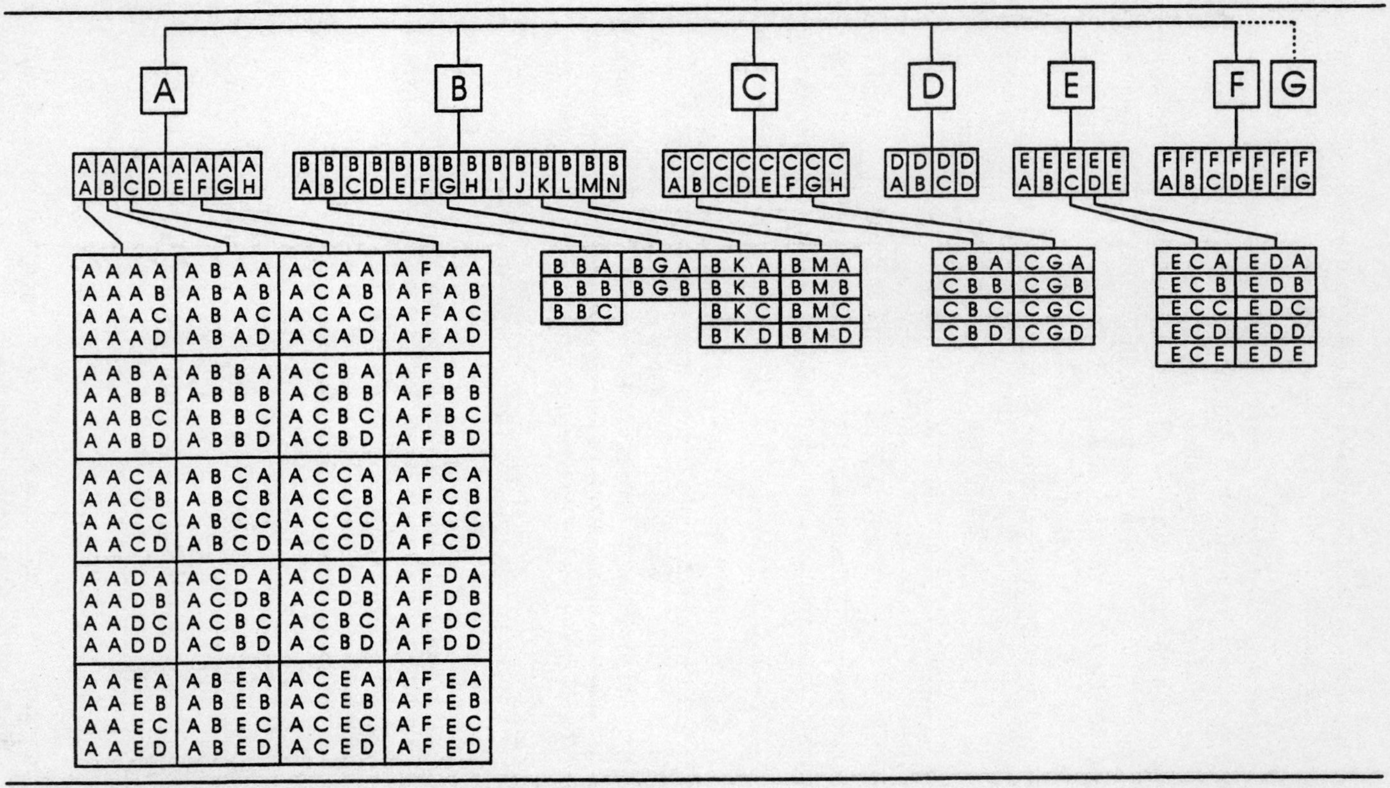

Figure 6: Value Tree: Los Angeles School Desegregation Plans

here. The total number of twigs (bottom locations of the value tree) depicted in Figure 6 was 144. This is one of the largest value trees we have seen. In fact, it is far too large. That seems to be a characteristic of most value trees built to evaluate important public programs. In part it is appropriate, since different values may be important to different stakeholders. But in part it represents the familiar process of losing perspective when passions are engaged. The larger the set of attributes, the less important each will be as a rule. Consequently, keeping the attribute list as short as the circumstances permit is an aid to perspective—and also an aid to the intelligibility and simplicity of the analysis.

We have neither had much success ourselves nor seen much in other uses of MAUT in keeping attribute lists short for public decisions especially political ones. But if all major stakeholders can sit around a conference table and work in reasonable harmony on pruning excessively bushy value trees, the result is often very good. Nice work—if you can accomplish it.

Comment

This is one of the longer chapters in this manual, a necessity due to the complexity and importance of the topic. MAUT evaluation begins with the identification of the stakeholders and the listing of the value attributes. We reiterate: If possible, keep the number of attributes small. Our technical experience indicates that eight would be about right and fifteen would already be excessive. However, as some of the examples in this chapter indicate, keeping the number of attributes small is difficult.

The major technical problem that arises with a large number of attributes is that the importance weights to be assigned to the attributes will often end up very small and thus blunt the meaningfulness of the weights. The next chapter discusses the problem of weighting.

Summary

Chapter 3 concentrates on the problem of identifying the stakeholders and eliciting the value attributes from them. A distinction is made between *actors,* people who make decisions about programs and perhaps take direct action to change programs, and people who are affected or impinged on by the program, either directly or indirectly. Both are important stakeholders, but they have different roles. Techniques for eliciting the value attributes from stakeholders are discussed and illustrated. The structuring of the value attributes into a value tree is demonstrated and the problem of multiple stakeholders with perhaps different value structures is discussed. The advantage of having a common value structure is emphasized, but a common structure is not a necessity to carry out a successful MAUT.

Often, differences between stakeholders can be described as differences in weights assigned to the attributes. When value attributes are formulated as program objectives, measures of how well these objectives have been obtained have to be defined. A specific example is given for the Community Anti-Crime (CAC) Program. Two other examples of identifying stakeholders, eliciting value attributes from them, and structuring those attributes are given from evaluations in civil justice and school desegregation.

4. WEIGHTING VALUE ATTRIBUTES

Why Weight?

Not all attributes are likely to be considered equally important. The function of weights is to express the importance of each attribute relative to all others. The weighting procedures we describe shortly vary in difficulty and in precision. But some form of weighting is usually essential. Weights capture the essence of value judgments. They can be expected to vary from stakeholder to stakeholder; indeed, stakeholders usually contribute only two kinds of judgments to MAUT analyses: attributes and weights. In most evaluations, incidentally, the fact that multiple stake holders are involved means that you cannot hope to elicit attributes and weights in the same session. Your first elicitation session will be concerned with attributes; after you have elicited all attributes and combined them into (we hope) one value tree, you will need to visit each stakeholder representative again in order to elicit weights on that tree.

Weights should, of course, reflect the purpose of the evaluation. The weights on administrative smoothness and efficiency, for example, might well be higher for an evaluation intended for monitoring or for programmatic fine tuning than for a full-scale impact evaluation—though that attribute would be relevant to both. Although the generalization is too simple, it is appealing to think of just two kinds of weights; one relevant to program management decisions, and the other relevant to impact assessment, current or prospective.

Values are reflected in weights, and values change over time. So weights should be reelicited in situations in which a program is periodically reevaluated. Since the program is designed around the old weights, it is relevant to evaluate it against both the old weights and the new ones.

In the kind of complex multilevel evaluation of the CAC example in chapter 3, it would be inappropriate to elicit all weights from one set of respondents. Different respondents function at different levels of the program. Legislators, for example, are interested in broad programmatic goals at the top of the value tree. Local project administrators, such as the director of the Midwood-Kings Development Corporation, are naturally concerned with the project-specific values relevant to their own projects. The question of who should assess which weights is a matter of evaluative judgment. The principle is obvious: Each stakeholder should judge weights in the level or levels of the tree in which he or she has knowledge, expertise, or interest. Translating that general principle into specific decisions can be sensitive, and it is not subject to specific rules that we know of.

The remainder of this chapter discusses various ways of eliciting weights. While we clearly prefer one way, *ratio weighting,* to its alternatives, we also know that it is a nuisance, and that simple alternatives to it often give essentially equivalent results. That is why we offer simpler alternatives. Those familiar with the very large literature of weighting will recognize that many different weighting procedures, even including equal weights, can often lead to equivalent aggregate utilities, or at least to the same ordering of options. If aggregate utilities are the goal of the analysis, easy procedures may work well, and demand much less effort of respondents. But for such purposes as monitoring and fine tuning, weights at lower levels of the value tree are much more important than for obtaining fully aggregated utilities. Moreover, the weights themselves may be useful information to those concerned with project or program management, since they indicate what stakeholders are most concerned about in a quantitative way.

Equal or Unit Weighting

The easiest weighting scheme is to assign equal or unit weights to each of the attributes, in other words, treat all attributes as equally important. While we do not recommend this scheme, we mention it for the following reasons: (1) it eliminates the problem of deciding what the weights should be and also eliminates the difficult task of obtaining the importance weight judgments from the stakeholders; (2) if wildly differing weights are obtained from conflicting stakeholders, then assigning equal weights is one way of resolving the disagreement; (3) a MAUT analysis always includes a sensitivity analysis, that is, a study is done to see how the final result is affected by changes in the weights, the location measures, the number of attributes used, and so on. One thing to try in a sensitivity analysis is equal weights. Chapter 7 shows how such sensitivity analyses are conducted.

Weights from Ranks

The simplest way of assessing differential weights is to arrange attributes in simple rank order, listing the most important attribute first, the least important attribute last, and the other attributes arranged from high to low between these two extremes. A numerical weight is then assigned to each attribute according to its rank in the list. The two most common ways to assign the numerical weights for the ranked attributes are:

(1) Assign the largest rank number to the most important attribute, the next highest number to the second most important attribute, and so on down the list until the least important attribute receives the rank of 1 (such numbers are called *inverse ranks*). Then add these numbers and divide each by the sum. The procedure of dividing each number by the sum of the numbers is called *normalizing*. It assures that the normalized numbers sum to 1. This final result is called *rank sum weighting*.

(2) Assign the numerical value of 1 to the most important attribute, 2 to the next most important attribute, and so on; the least important attribute receives a rank of N where N is the number of attributes. The reciprocal or 1 divided by each of the numbers so assigned is then taken, and these reciprocals are normalized. This assures that the most important attribute receives the highest numerical weight and the least important attribute receives the lowest weight. This is called *rank reciprocal weighting*. It requires a little more arithmetic than rank weights, but is easy to do.

In any method based on ranks, you must consider the possibility of tied ranks. Suppose that the ranks that would originally have been assigned the numbers 3, 4, and 5 are tied. Then all three of them receive the number 4. The number is used in rank sum weighting, and its reciprocal is used in rank reciprocal weighting. If 3 and 4 had been tied, each would have received a rank of 3.5.

These two weighting schemes can be illustrated with a numerical example. Refer back to Table 5 (chapter 2). This lists the twigs and gives their weights for the drug counseling center siting example. We can rearrange them in order of decreasing original weight, assign them ranks, and calculate rank sum and rank reciprocal weights for them (see Table 10).

Obviously, any rank weighting method is at best an approximation. Inspection of Table 10 shows that the rank sum weights are far flatter than the rank reciprocal weights. Since the original weights were quite flat themselves, the rank sum procedure produces an excellent approximation to them, while the rank reciprocal procedure does not. Had the original weights been less flat (as they typically are), the rank reciprocal procedure would have produced the better approximation. Unfortunately, if you already know the appropriate weights, there is no point in using an approximation, while if you do not, you cannot be sure which to use. If the stakeholder has some feeling for whether the proper weights are relatively flat or relatively steep, one might simply choose between these approximations on the basis of that feeling, and accept the results of the approxi-

TABLE 10
An Illustration of Rank Weighting Techniques

Rank Label	Original Weight	Inverse Rank	Rank Sum Weight	Normal Rank	Reciprocal of Normal Rank	Rank Reciprocal Weight
AA	.168	12	.154	1	1	.326
BA	.120	10.5	.135	2.5	.400	.131
BB	.120	10.5	.135	2.5	.400	.131
CA	.099	9	.115	4	.250	.082
AB	.090	7.5	.096	5.5	.182	.059
DA	.090	7.5	.096	5.5	.182	.059
CB	.061	6	.077	7	.143	.047
AC	.060	4.5	.058	8.5	.118	.039
AD	.060	4.5	.058	8.5	.118	.039
AE	.052	3	.038	10	.100	.033
DB	.050	2	.026	11	.091	.030
CC	.030	1	.013	12	.083	.027
Sums	1.000	78	1.002		3.067	1.001

mation. In any case, the stakeholder will have to arrange the things to be weighted in rank order, and to make judgments about ties.

Ratio Weighting

This method begins as with the previous methods, i.e., the attributes are first placed in rank order of importance such that the most important attribute is at the top of the list and the least important is at the bottom of the list. The *least* important attribute is then assigned a value of ten (10). The stakeholder then assigns numerical weights such that the next in the list (from the bottom) gets a value depicting how much more important that attribute is relative to the least important attribute. Thus if a value of 20 is assigned, it means that that attribute is twice as important as the least important (which received a value of 10). The stakeholder works up the list of attributes assigning numerical values in a similar fashion. Thus if some other attribute receives a value of 40, it is considered four times as important as the least important attribute (which received a value of 10), and twice as important as the attribute that received a value of 20. The stakeholder should be carefully instructed about what the weights mean using this method. Ties are permitted, i.e., if the expert thinks two or more attributes are equal in importance they would receive the same numerical weight. Since this method is more demanding than the rank methods, it is often a good idea to give the stakeholder an example of how the method works before he or she proceeds to make judgments. This is particularly important if the weights are being elicited from the stakeholder via mail questionnaires. The example given in Table 11 is quite useful. Again, we use the siting example, this time confining our attention to its four top-level values. In order of judged importance, they are: (A) good conditions for staff, (B) easy access for clients, (C) suitability of space for the center's functions, and (D) administrative convenience.

Table 11 assigns a reference weight of 10 to the least important attribute, administrative convenience (D). The other attributes are then judged relative to that one. The numbers entered in Table 11 are as they would be elicited from individual stakeholders. Thus we will have a set of ratio weights for each stakeholder. Left to their own devices, people tend in this procedure to make judgments that end in 5 or 0, which does little harm, though people should be encouraged to think about their judgments and to make as careful discriminations as their feelings permit.

Consistency Check: Use of the Triangular Table

If possible, the evaluator should work with individual stakeholders, or groups of them if they are making group judgments, when the ratio method is used. If so, the triangular table included in Table 12 is useful in encouraging consistency. The stakeholder first makes the judgments in the first column. If D has a weight of 10, what weight should C have so that the ratio of C to D seems appropriate? The answer 15, for example, would mean that C is 1 1/2 times as important as D; the answer 20 would mean that C is twice as important as D, and so on. After that judgment has been made for C, the next judgment is the ratio of B to D. After that, A to D. Then the stakeholder moves over to the next column, which ignores D and assigns a weight of 10 to C, and makes the ratio judgments of A and B to C. Finally, the stakeholder does the same for the third column. The final column is calculated by normalizing the numbers in column 1.

All entries in a table such as Table 12 should be consistent. If, for example, a stakeholder has made the indicated judgments in column 1, and then in column 2 judged the ratio of B to C to be 20 to 10 (2 to 1), the evaluator would point out the inconsistency between that judgment and the numbers in column 1, and invite the stakeholder to revise either or both judgments to ensure consistency. Only after all the judgments have been made consistently should the normalized weights be calculated. It is preferable to do that calculation while the stakeholder is still present, so that he or she can consider the weights that result from his or her judgments, decide whether or not they seem appropriate, and if not, go back and revise the ratios.

If the number of values to be compared with one another exceeds six or seven, the number of ratio judgments required to complete a full triangular

TABLE 11

Example: Evaluating Sites

Step 1	Step 2	Step 3
Review list of value attributes. (An attribute = a "thing to consider")	Rank order the value attributes to reflect their relative importance to you as you evaluate location sites. Ties are acceptable. Enter the letter corresponding to the most important attribute listed in Step 1 on line 1. Enter the second most important on line 2, and so on. If any two attributes are equally important, place both letters on the same line. For three-way ties place three letters on the same line, and so on.	Weight the value attributes. Assign 10 points to the least important attribute and then indicate your own opinion about the relative importance of each attribute by assigning weights accordingly. (No upper limit on weights)

Value Attributes	Rank Order		Assign Weights
	Line 1 A	(Most important)	40
	Line 2 B	....	30 Suitability of Space (C) is twice as
	Line 3 C	....	20 important as Administrative Convenience (D)
A. Good conditions for staff	Line 4 D	(Least important)	10
B. Easy access for client			10 points assigned as reference
C. Suitability of space			to least important attributes
D. Administrative convenience			For this person Good conditions (A) is twice as important as Suitability of Space (C) and four times as important as Administrative Convenience (D).

57

TABLE 12
The Triangular Table for Ratio Weighting: Check for Consistency

Attribute Label	1 Ratios to 4	2 Ratios to 3	3 Ratios to 2	4 Weights[1]
A	31	22	18	.43
B	17	12	10	.24
C	14	10		.19
D	10			.14
Sums	72			1.00

1. These are the normalized weights of the values given in Column 1.

table can get tediously large (six values requires ten judgments, seven requires fifteen, and so on). In that case, it may be appropriate to reduce the amount of judgmental labor by using only the first two columns. But at least one column other than the first should ordinarily be filled out to provide for at least some consistency checking.

If two values are originally judged to be tied, then of course, there is no point in judging ratios in both columns in which they receive 10s; either one will do.

The other function of the triangular table of judgments is to take care of the case in which the least important attribute is considered by the stakeholder to be utterly unimportant, deserving a weight of 0. In that case, the initial set of judgments should be made in the first column in which a nonzero value receives a weight of 10, and all values below that should get weights of 0.

A More Realistic Example

We now give a more realistic example of the ratio method of assigning importance weights, one selected from an actual evaluation study—the evaluation of a program for resolving landlord/tenant disputes, the Office of the Rentalsman (OR) example alluded to in the previous chapter. In that particular study, sixteen attributes were identified. The instruments used to elicit importance weights from the stakeholders are given in Figure 7 and Table 13. Figure 7 gives the instructions and Table 13 is the sheet on which the stakeholder gave his/her weights. As in the previous example, the attributes are listed along the side with their respective definitions. The numbers written in under the assigned weights column of Table 13 are the ones actually obtained from one of the participants in this particular

Name _____
(PLEASE PRINT)

This is the second phase of this process. Part 11 asks for your views about the relative importance of 16 attributes considered important to the operation and administration of the Rentalsman's office as it is operating in British Columbia.

On Page 3, you will find the 16 attributes listed. We would like you to review this list and then indicate your views as to the relative importance of each attribute on the list as follows:

1. Please consider the 16 attributes (and only these 16) and then RANK ORDER them in decreasing order of importance to you, with number 1 being most important, and the least important last. (Ties are acceptable).
2. Once you have rank-ordered them, please reflect on their relative importance to you. How much weight does each attribute carry relative to the other attributes as you would use them to appraise an office such as the Office of Rentalsman?

Please write the weights you would assign to each attribute to reflect its relative importance to you.

a. Do this by assigning a weight of *10* to the least important attribute (lowest rank) as a common starting point.
b. Next, for the attribute with the next higher rank, assign it a weight to reflect its importance compared to the lowest attribute. For example, it may be half again as important to you as the lowest attribute. If so, it would receive a weight of 15. If it is twice as important, it would receive a weight of 20.
c. Then go to the next most important attribute and compare it to the one just completed and repeat the process.

An attribute with a weight of 40 is twice as important as one with 20 and half as important as one with 80, and so on. An attribute with 50 is as important as one with 20 and one with 30 *taken together*.

There are no limits to the weight you assign. When finished, you will have weighted all the attributes to reflect their relative importance to you. Page 2 shows a simplified example of how this is done.[1]

Remember, we are interested in your personal preferences, so there are no "right" or "wrong" answers. The definitions of each attribute are given for guidance only. You are free to redefine them in any way you wish.

Figure 7: Instructions for Eliciting Weights via the Ratio Method
1. The example is the one similar to that given in Table 11.

TABLE 13

Illustration of the Form Used to Elicit Importance Weights via the Ratio Method

Appraising Programs to Handle Landlord-Tenant Relations

Step 1.	Step 2.	Step 3.
Review the following value attributes in terms of their importance in appraising a Rentalsman Office. You may provide your own definitions if you wish.	Rank order the value attributes to reflect their relative importance to you as you appraise the Rentalsman's Office. Enter the letter corresponding to the most important attribute listed in Step 1 on Line 1. Enter the second most important on Line 2 and so on. If any two attributes are equally important, place both letters on the same line. For three-way ties, place three letters on the same line, and so on.	Weight the value attributes. Assign 10 points to the *least* important attribute and then indicate your own opinion about the relative importance of each attribute by assigning weights accordingly. (No upper limit on weights.)

ATTRIBUTE	Definition	Rank Order	Assign Weights
A. SPEED	The length of time the institution takes to provide information and process disputes.	Line 1 K	170
B. POWER	The ease with which the institution can enforce the orders which it issues.		
C. VISIBILITY	The extent to which citizens are aware of the Office and its function.	Line 2 D	160
D. FAIRNESS	The extent to which the process reflects natural justice and general equity.	Line 3 I	120
E. ACCESSIBILITY	Ease of registering requests and complaints; taking into consideration procedural complexity; hr./days available, and physical location.	Line 4 P	110

F. EDUCATION—The degree to which the institution provides information to members of the public about their rights, obligations, and remedies to disputes.

G. INVESTIGATIVE POWER—The extent to which the institution takes responsibility for investigating.

H. INFORMALITY—The degree to which the dispute process does not follow a prescribed pattern, style.

I. INDEPENDENCE/ACCOUNTABILITY—The degree and consistency with which the institution's behavior is directly influenced by other institution's (e.g., electorate, ministry, private associations, public opinion).

J. FLEXIBILITY—The degree to which the institution's decisions reflect the circumstances of the particular parties involved in disputes.

K. IMPARTIALITY—The extent to which decisions do not give special consideration to either landlords or tenants or to any irrelevant attributes of any disputants.

L. EXPERTISE—The degree to which the institution is familiar with the types of disputes and questions generally submitted to it.

M. JURISDICTION—The degree to which jurisdictional limitations on the institution's operations are a problem for the parties involved in disputes.

N. COST—Cost in dollars or dollar-equivalents (e.g., time) for the individuals to secure the services of the institution.

O. EXPENSE—Cost to the institution for providing the services which it provides.

P. CONSISTENCY—The degree to which the institution's decisions reflect general rules.

Line 5 A, E 100
Line 6 G 75
Line 7 N 60
Line 8 L 55
Line 9 J, H 50
Line 10 B 40
Line 11 C 25
Line 12 M 20
Line 13 O, E 10
Line 14 ___ ......
Line 15 ___ ......
Line 16 ___ ......

evaluation study. Thus, this particular stakeholder thought that attribute K, *impartiality,* was the most important attribute and it received an importance weight of 170, which is 17 times as important as the least important attributes of *expense* (O) and *accessibility* (E). The second most important attribute is that of *fairness* (D), which received a weight of 160, and so on.

An Aid to Ratio Weighting: Use of the Value Tree

If there are many twigs, then ratio weighting can be quite time consuming and demanding of the stakeholders. One technique to help the stakeholder is to have him or her use the value tree of the attributes if such a tree has been constructed. Have each stakeholder first judge ratio weights for the main branches of the tree and then under each branch obtain the ratio weights for the subattributes, making separate sets of judgments for each lower-level group of values under an upper-level value. The result was illustrated in Figure 1 (chapter 2). When these weights are normalized, then the weight for each twig of the tree is easily obtained by multiplication down through the value tree. As an illustration, consider Table 14, which lists the attributes for the value tree of Figure 5 (chapter 3). There are four major attributes: *resolution process* (A), *action process* (B), *administrative process* (C), *and financial process* (D). The experts can be asked to make ratio weight judgments for these four attributes, resulting (as an example) in normalized weights of (. 47)A; (. 17)B; (. 30)C; and (.06)D, respectively. Then under each of these the expert can also make the ratio weight judgments, resulting (as an example) under B, in the normalized weights of (.38)BA; (.31)BB; and (.31)BC. To obtain the final weight for each attribute at each twig, multiply these two numbers. Thus AA *fairness* receives a final weight of 11 (.47 X .24 = . 11). As mentioned previously (chapter 2), this is called *multiplying through the tree.*

Comment

We recommend that if at all possible the ratio weighting method be used. Since this requires the stakeholders to rank order the attributes in order of importance, this will yield three possible weighting schemes (rank weights, rank reciprocals, and ratio sum weights).

Assignment of Weights by Multiple Stakeholders

The use of the MAUT model, which often represents the viewpoints of multiple stakeholders, requires the assignment of weights to the value attributes reflecting each attribute's importance. Using the methods de-

TABLE 14
An Example of Ratio Weighting Using the Value Tree[1]

(.47) A Resolution Process	(.17) B Action Process	(.30) C Administrative Process	(0. 06) D Financial Process
(.24) AA Fairness (.11)	(.38) BA Power (.07) (to enforce decisions)	(.29) BA Accessibility (.09)	(.63) DA Cost (.04) (to the individual)
(.24) AB Impartiality (.11)	(.31) BB Investigative Power (.05)	(.25) CB Education (.07)	(.37) DB Expense (.02) (to the institution)
(.13) AC Expertise (.06)	(.31) BC Independence/Accountability (.05)	(.23) CC Visibility (.07)	
(.13) AD Flexibility (.O6)		(.23) CD Speed (.07)	
(.13) AE Consistency (.06)			
(.11) AF Jurisdiction (.05)			
(.09) AG Information (.04)			

1. The value attributes were those elicited by the expert stakeholders concerned with the evaluation of the Office of the Rentalsman.

scribed in this chapter, we arrive at a set of weights for each stakeholder. Should these individual weights be averaged? The answer is yes but we do not recommend replacing the individual weights with the average. Use the average as another set of weights and carry through the analysis to be explained in chapter 6 using each stakeholder's weights as well as the average weight. The question of interest is whether the average leads to aggregate utilities substantially different in rank order from those of the individual stakeholders. Often, the answer will be "no." Of course it is always desirable, if possible, to arrive at a consensus on what the weights should be. If the stakeholders can be brought together in a group they can often arrive at such a consensus. The presentation of the value tree to the group is often useful in aiding this process. When the stakeholders represent different groups with different ideas about what attributes are most important it is often possible for each group to specify its own weights, but no attempt is made to amalgamate the separate group weightings.

Another approach is for groups essentially to negotiate among themselves to arrive at an "agreed-to" set of weights. For instance, groups may jointly decide that each of them should receive equal weight in an overall sense, so that the weights used in the MAUT model are averages of the weights assigned by each separate group. Such weights normally will not reflect the values of any one individual. Rather, models using such weights are essentially models of policy, jointly formulated by multiple groups or individuals. Thus, just as policies are the result of group consensus, MAUT models that reflect policy also result from group consensus—in this case, regarding the appropriate weights to use.

Summary

Chapter 4 discusses the problem of weighting the value attributes so that they are arranged in numerical order of importance. Several different techniques for weighting are described in detail and examples of each method are given. Emphasis is on simplicity in weight elicitation from the stakeholders. Special forms that have been used to successfully elicit weights are provided and a way to check on the consistency of weight judgments is given. How to use the value tree as a technique to simplify the weighting process is explained and illustrated by a concrete example.

If possible, it is always desirable to arrive at a consensus on what the weights should be. If the stakeholders can be brought together in a group, they can often arrive at such a consensus. The presentation of the value tree (if one has been constructed) to the group is helpful in aiding this process. But it is not always possible to work with groups. When stakeholders represent different groups with different ideas about which attributes are most important, it is often possible for each group to specify its own weights, but no attempt is made to amalgamate the separate group weightings. Replacing individual weights with a single average is not recommended. The chapter concludes with a discussion of the problems of assignment of weights by multiple stakeholders.

5. THE LOCATION MEASURES

This chapter discusses and illustrates how location measures for each attribute are determined for each of the options or entities to be evaluated.

First, a few reminders about ideas from previous chapters. A location measure is an assessment of how desirable an option is with respect to a particular twig or bottom node of a value tree. This is expressed as a number technically called a utility. Throughout this chapter, we use the words "location measure" and "utility" interchangeably, though our procedures differ from classical ones for utility measurement.

Such numbers, since they are assessments of desirability on single attributes of evaluation, are in principle subjective—but in fact may be either simple arithmetical transformations on objective measures or basically impressionistic judgments. We distinguish between the two cases. The first arises when some objective measure captures what you consider the attribute to be concerned with; in that case, your task is to transform the number so that it is comparable in meaning to other numbers. The second arises when the attribute is inherently judgmental, as office attractiveness was in the Drug Free Center siting example. Such judgments, sometimes made by program people or others close to the program and sometimes by independent and presumably impartial experts, ordinarily need no transformations, since they are already on a scale that makes them comparable to all other measures of desirability.

Linear Measures

We consider the first kind of instance first. In the Drug Free Center siting example, one attribute was office size. The natural unit in which this attribute is measured is square feet. From chapter 2, you may recall that the director assigned a utility of 0 to an office 60 square feet in size, and a utility 100 to an office 160 square feet in size. Since more size is preferable to less, and we are confining ourselves to linear functions relating desirability to physical measures, whenever, in this case desirability either continuously increases or continuously decreases with the physical measure over the whole range; it follows that a 140 square feet office would have a location measure of 80.

A simple graphic representation of this is given in Figure 8. The horizontal (X) axis of Figure 8 is the range of the attribute in its "natural units,"

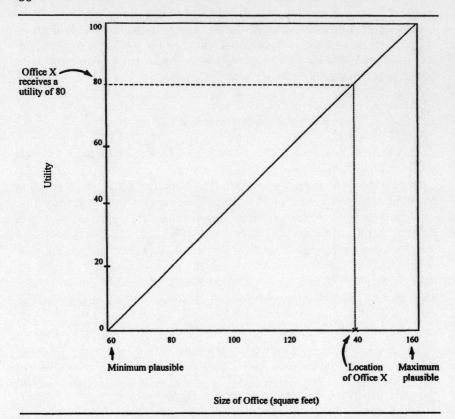

Figure 8:   Example of Simple Linear Graph Relating Subjective Value (Utility) to Physical Atrribute Location (office size in square feet)

going from the lowest plausible value to the highest plausible value. The vertical (Y) axis goes from 0 to 100. To assign utility simply locate the option on the X axis and "read off" its utility on the Y axis.

If the simple linear relationship between utility and the attribute's natural units as indicated in Figure 8 is acceptable, then there is even an easier way to assign utilities. The calculation is simple: for an office size of 140 sq. ft. it is:

$$80 = 100 (140 - 60)/(160 - 60)$$

More generally, if L_A is the actual location measure, L_{min} is the minimum value, and L_{max} is the maximum value, the calculation is:

$$\text{Location of } L_A = 100 (L_A - L_{min})/(L_{max} - L_{min}) \qquad [1]$$

Consider another example. One attribute of programs intend to reduce juvenile crime might be: *average number of arrests per offender per year.* The natural unit for this attribute is obvious. Its minimum is obviously 0, and that has a utility of 100. Choice of a number to assign utility 0 to is a judgment; it might be 10 or more. In that example, less is preferable to more, so the equation appropriate to the problem is no longer equation 1. Instead it is:

$$\text{Location of } L_A = 100 \, (L_{max} - L_A)/(L_{max} - L_{min}) \qquad [2]$$

To be sure you are with us, use equation 2 to verify that an average of seven arrests per offender per year should get a location measure of 30.

Equation 1, then, is appropriate if more is better than less, and equation 2 is appropriate if less is better than more.

Ranges and Outside-Range Locations

In these examples, some judgmental inputs were necessary because the limits defining utilities of 0 and 100 were judgments. In some cases, no such judgments may be needed. For example, the attribute *percentage of arrests that result in court appearances* seems to have a natural range from 0% to 100%. But such natural ranges may be deceptive. Recall from chapter 2 that we emphasized the importance of making the boundaries realistic. Is it realistic to expect anything like 100% of juvenile arrests to lead to court appearances? If not, you should assign a more realistic upper bound.

In chapter 2 we discussed the nature of such upper and lower bounds. We said then and reiterate now, that they should be minimum and maximum plausible values, rather than minimum and maximum possible, conceivable, or actual values. The fact that we choose a range not directly controlled by the actual locations we are using (if in fact we know them) means that every now and then an instance will fall outside the range. We gave an example in chapter 2, in which the center director assigned a location measure of 100 to having the bus stop no more than a block from the center, and 0 to having it four blocks away. We said in chapter 2 that on that scale a site with a bus stop five blocks away would score -29 in utility. A simple substitution into equation 2 will now permit you to calculate this number for yourself. The natural unit of measurement is half-blocks; the minimum is one, and the maximum is eight. So the calculation is:

$$100 \, (8 - 10)/(8 - 1) = -200/7 = -28.57.$$

While such outside-the-range objects of evaluation can occur for both objectively measurable and judgmental twigs, they should present no special problems so long as the meaning of the ranges is kept clearly in mind. Remember that an alternative approach to outside-the-range cases is to treat them as though they fell as the range boundary; whether to do this or instead to use a number less than 0 or greater than 100 is a judgmental question, and depends on whether you consider the difference between the boundary value and the value observed to make any meaningful difference to the attractiveness of the option.

Judgmental Location Measures

Purely judgmental location measures present no arithmetical problems, since nothing like equation 1 or 2 need be used. However, they may present problems because judges may be reluctant to approach the extremes closely, especially the lower extreme. Judges of location measures should keep two things in mind: first, that the location measures serve to differentiate one object of evaluation from another, and so should be well spread out, and second, that assignments of both 0 and 100 should be realistic with respect to the evaluation in hand, not with respect to the attribute in general. Judgmental assessments of self-discipline appropriate to selecting candidates for West Point, for example, would almost certainly be quite inappropriate for selecting candidates for release from a juvenile detention center. The attribute of evaluation (self-discipline) might be the same, but the ranges of it that one would expect to encounter are entirely different for the two examples.

Although in the siting example we had the director serving as judge of the location measures, that is not generally good practice. Evaluations gain in objectivity and credibility if judgmental assessments are made by experts on the topic of the assessment, preferably experts not too closely tied to the program being evaluated. If different twigs call for differing kinds of expertise, use of more than one outside expert is usually wise. Indeed, it is exactly in assessing judgmental location measures that we consider independent expertise to have its most important role. If those closely associated with a program disagree with externally assessed location measures, they can make independent assessments of their own and then report the consequences of using them instead of the outside ones as an ingredient of the sensitivity analysis.

Bilinear Location Measures

Some location measures do grow out of measurements or counts, but do not have the convenient property either that more is better than less or less is better than more. Sometimes, an intermediate value will be "just right," and deviations from it in either direction will be less attractive. The standard example is the amount of sugar in a cup of coffee. If you like two spoonfuls, you will find none too few and four too many. But, in the example, the function is not symmetric for most of us; most people who like sugar in their coffee prefer too much to too little.

We find it convenient to approximate such utility functions by two lines rather than one. One of those two lines will run from 0 at either the minimum or maximum value to 100 at the optimal value. But the other one ordinarily will not descend from the optimal value all the way to 0 again. A judge considering a sentencing decision might provide an example. The legally specified boundaries for the decision might be 1 to 5 years. The judge might, for a defendant, feel that 4 years is just right, and that 1 year is so inadequate as to deserve a utility value of 0. So the utility value of any sentence between 1 and 4 years would be given by equation 1, with 1 as L_{min} and 4 as L_{max}. But the judge might well feel that a 5-year sentence deserves a utility value of, say, 60. In that case, how would the judge assess a 4 1/2-year sentence? Intuition suggests 80, and calculation can confirm it. The appropriate equation is an adaption of equation 2, with L_{max} being the location measure associated with the maximum sentence, in this case 5 years. The equation is

$$\text{Location of } L_A = U_{max} + (100 - U_{max}) \times (L_{max} - L_A)/(L_{max} - L_{min}) \qquad [3]$$

Note that in this example L_{min} is the location of the peak; in this case 4 years. What equation 3 does, of course, is to partition the location measure into two parts, U_{max} (60 in this example), and the difference between U_{max} and 100. It automatically awards U_{max}, and then increases it by the proportion of the remainder that corresponds to the proportionate distance between L_{max} and L_A. To make sure that the symbols are all clear, we work the example problem:

$$\text{Location of } LA = 60 + (100 - 60) (5 - 4.5)/(5 - 4) = 80$$

It could also happen that the lower, rather than the upper, branch of the bilinear utility function did not hit 0 utility. In that case, the equation corresponding to equation 3 would be:

$$\text{Location of } L_A = U_{min} + (100 - U_{min}) \times (L_A - L_{min})/(L_{max} - L_{min}) \qquad [4]$$

Note that in equation 4, L_{max} is now the location of the peak.

Nonlinear Location Measures

Our use of linear and bilinear location measures is, as we pointed out in chapter 2, an enormous simplification, very much out of the spirit of formal decision analysis. Our justification for doing it is straightforward. If your desirability or utility function increases steadily or decreases steadily, or has one interior maximum, then this approximation will work so well that there is little point in using anything more sophisticated. If the approximation reverses an evaluative ordering compared with some other form of location measure elicitation, it will be because the options being ordered are so close to each other in attractiveness that fluctuations in weight or location measure judgments would also be enough to change orderings, and consequently no strong conclusions about ordering would be justifiable in any case.

However, if your intuition is severely violated by thinking of your assessments of desirability as expressible by one or at most two straight lines, you have a rather simple alternative. You can simply draw a graph with the physical measure on the X axis, the 0 to 100 scale on the Y axis, and draw whatever function most appeals to you in that graph. Drawing a graph is obviously mandatory in the very rare case in which your utility function has two or more peaks in it.

Choice Among Competing Location Measures

Especially in social conflict situations, one common topic of controversy is what location measures to use in an evaluation. An embattled program can live or die depending on whether it is evaluated primarily by looking at measures on which it is doing poorly or on measures on which it is doing well. We discussed the issue in chapter 3, using the nuclear power debate as an example. Those who wish to defend nuclear power would like the expected deaths following an accident to be measured as expected fatalities—a quite low number. Those who wish to oppose it want to use deaths following the maximum credible accident for the same purpose—and that is a much larger number.

The only reason we bring this up again here is to reiterate the suggestion of chapter 3. From a MAUT point of view, if there is no good reason for preferring one such measure to another, why not use both? Then the conflict over which measure is appropriate becomes a conflict about which twig of a value tree to weight heavily. This does not eliminate the conflict but it reduces it to the familiar form that, in our view, characterizes virtually every evaluative conflict we have seen: disagreement, not about values, their structures, or about possible measures, but rather disagreement about weights.

The Relation Between Location Measures and Weights

In chapter 4, on weighting, we never really explained what a weight was. Our reason for not doing so was that, although we could and did use evocative words like "importance," we could give no precise definition until we had discussed location measures. The two concepts are very closely intertwined.

A weight is an exchange rate among location measures. Suppose, for example, that you assign a weight of .5 to attribute A and a weight of .25 to attribute B. A is thus twice as "important" as B (.50/.25 = 2). You are then implicitly saying that, if all other attributes are held constant, you would be willing to pay two utility units of attribute B to gain one of attribute A. Or, to put it the other way around, you would pay half a utility unit of attribute A to gain a full utility unit of attribute B.

It is for this reason that judges of weights need to know the maximum and minimum location values of each attribute. They also should understand the idea that weights are exchange rates. The reason for this is that once a weight is assigned to an attribute it is always for a given range of location measures. If the range of such measures should change, the weights should change accordingly. Attributes with location measures that are reduced to a very narrow range from minimum to maximum plausible should receive lower weights relative to the other attributes and vice versa.

We recognize that the interpretation of weights as exchange rates among location measures is a subtle idea. In working with stakeholders who are assigning importance weights we explain it by giving examples such as that of the second previous paragraph.

Fortunately, this formal interpretation corresponds quite closely to our intuitive understanding of the word "importance." It seems natural to say that we will give up a lot on an unimportant attribute to gain a little on an important one. This discussion does no more than to give that natural thought quantitative form. It is also fortunate that the relationship between importance weights and location measures will not create a problem if the range of the location measures is chosen carefully in the first place, and then *left alone*. From a practical standpoint, it is better to have an option with location measures outside the original range receive utilities outside the 0-100 range than to try to figure out how to fix up the weights to adjust for a range change.

COLLECTING LOCATION MEASURES

As with most MAUT procedures, we consider it wise to elicit location measures from individual respondents or small groups if possible. Procedures for value and weight elicitation are sufficiently demanding that we are rather skeptical about mail-and-return procedures for carrying them out. But location measures are sometimes easier to elicit, depending on how subjective they are, how willing the respondents are to take time and thought in assessing them, and on the nature and complexity of the dimensions on which they must be assessed. Any of the procedures we have proposed in this chapter are at least conceivable as mail-and-return procedures—with the proviso that simple linear procedures are so simple that the respondent may wonder what they are for.

THE OFFICE OF THE RENTALSMAN EXAMPLE

In chapter 2 we discussed the evaluation of the Office of the Rentalsman. We return to it now to illustrate one way to deal with the problem of collecting location measures that make comparisons among programs possible when only one program exists.

In such cases, the natural evaluative strategy is to compare the program in place with an alternative to it—in this case, with the program it replaced, which was to handle landlord/tenant disputes in the courts.

That evaluation identified sixteen attributes; they were listed as Figure 5 (chapter 3). The evaluation was intended, among other purposes, to find out how satisfied or dissatisfied the respondents (all expert in such dispute resolution problems and closely familiar with the Office of the Rentalsman [OR] and with the court as an alternative to it) were.

Each respondent judged how well each attribute was being served by the OR now, how well it should be served, and how well it had been served by the court system that the OR had replaced. As an illustration of how this was done, consider the attribute of *visibility*. Each expert was presented with the following:

VISIBILITY

The extent to which the citizens are aware of the Office and its function.

1. How much visibility exists now in the OR?
   (min) 1 2 3 4 5 6 7 (max)

2. How much visibility should exist in the OR?
   (min) 1 2 3 4 5 6 7 (max)

3. How much visibility do you think existed in the Court
   with respect to resolving landlord-tenant disputes prior
   to the establishment of the OR?
   (min) 1 2 3 4 5 6 7 (max)

This scale was repeated for all sixteen attributes. The expert was requested to give three ratings on a 7-point scale:

(1) How much of the attribute did he (she) think *actually* existed in the operation of the OR at the present time.

(2) How much of the attribute did he (she) think *should* be connected with the operation of the OR.

(3) How much of the attribute did he (she) think existed in the Provincial Small Claims Court with respect to resolving landlord/tenant disputes *prior* to the establishment of the OR.

The answer to the first of these questions can be interpreted as an estimate of how well the expert thought that particular attribute was being served in the OR. The answer to the second question compared to the answer to question 1 can be interpreted as an estimate of how much the expert thought that particular attribute should be increased or decreased in the operation of the OR. For example, if the expert gave a numerical response of 3 to question 1 and a 5 to question 2, that is an indication that that particular attribute's function should be increased.

The answer to the third question can be interpreted as an estimate of how well each expert thought that particular attribute was served in the court with respect to resolving landlord/tenant disputes. By comparing the answer to question 3 to that of question 1, we can obtain an estimate of satisfaction/dissatisfaction of using the OR versus using the court for handling landlord/tenant disputes. For example, if the expert gave a numerical response of 3 to question 1 and 5 to question 3, that is an indication that the court was "doing better" on that attribute than the OR. If the converse were true, then the expert thought the OR was functioning better on that attribute than the court.

Note, in this example, that the judgments provided by the experts on the three scales described above replaced the location (utility) values described earlier in this chapter and that they are on a 7-point scale, not a 100-point scale. However, the use of a 7-point scale was arbitrary, and it could have been replaced with a 100-point scale. Alternatively, equation 1 could be used to transformation location measures from the 7-point scale to a 0-100 scale. For a score of 3 on the 7-point scale, the arithmetic would be:

$$\text{Location} = 100(3 - 1)(7 - 1) = 33.33$$

The results of this particular evaluation will be given in chapter 6.

Summary

Chapter 5 discusses and illustrates how location measures for each attribute are determined for each option or entity to be evaluated. A location measure, also called single-attribute utility, is an assessment of how desirable an option is with respect to each of the value attributes. Simple graphic methods for assigning location measures on a common scale are illustrated. The simple equations giving the same answers as the graphic solution are also provided. All possible cases that are apt to arise in practical evaluations are demonstrated.

A somewhat technical but important discussion examines the relation between location measures and weights. A weight can be interpreted as an exchange rate among location measures. The reason for this is that once a weight is assigned to an attribute it is always for a given range of location measures for that attribute. If the range of such measures should change, then the weights should change accordingly.

The chapter concludes with an example of how to make comparisons among programs when a new program has replaced an older one and the evaluation examines whether the new program is better than the old program. A technique for assigning location measures for the current and prior programs is illustrated.

6. PUTTING IT ALL TOGETHER: THE AGGREGATION OF WEIGHTS AND UTILITIES

Through the techniques described in chapters 4 and 5 we have arrived at two sets of numbers: the importance weights, one for each attribute, usually normalized to sum to 1.0, and the utilities assigned to each decision alternative on each of the attributes usually (but not always) expressed on a scale from 0 to 100. The next step, to be described in this chapter, is to aggregate these two sets of numbers into one composite using an aggregation rule. Although the literature describes very complicated aggregation rules, we use only one because it is by far the simplest. The equation takes the following form:

$$U_j = \sum_{i=1}^{n} w_i u_{ij} \qquad [5]$$

where U_j is the overall or composite utility for the jth option such as a particular site or a particular delinquency treatment program; w_i is the normalized weight assigned to the ith attribute; and u_{ij} is the utility of the jth option on the ith attribute. The symbol Σ means to sum the weighted utilities over all the attributes from the first (1) to the last (n). We illustrated this arithmetic in the site selection example of chapter 2, and we refer the reader back to Table 5 in that chapter.

Equation 5 will yield a composite utility for each alternative using a particular set of weights and utilities. These can be averaged, of course, but we recommend that they also be kept separate so that each stakeholder's evaluation can be retained for analysis. The larger the numerical value of U, the "better"; thus whatever decision alternative receives the

TABLE 15
**Overall Weighted Utilities for the OR Now, How It Should Be,
and How It Was Prior to the OR (Court)**

	Utility Now	*Utility Should*	*Utility Prior (Court)*
Mean	434.1	599.7	425.3
Median	432.2	603.3	407.4
Standard Deviation	83.7	30.7	82.9
Range			
Minimum	312.7	547.2	275.5
Maximum	526.1	635.5	568.3

NOTE: The numbers in the Table are averaged over all 12 experts.

largest U should be considered the "best" under the procedure described in this manual. We turn now to examples of this aggregation process.

EXAMPLE: THE EVALUATION OF THE OFFICE OF THE RENTALSMAN (OR)

The Office of the Rentalsman (OR) described in chapter 3 was set up in Vancouver, British Columbia, to handle landlord/tenant disputes. It replaced the court as the means for resolving such disputes. This evaluation concentrated on having the experts "rate" the OR as it is operating now on each of the attributes; on how it *should* be operating; and how the court operated on each of the attributes *prior* to the creation of OR (see Table 5 in chapter 3). We will present three sets of results of this particular MAUT evaluation ranging from highly summarized (averages) down to individual "expert by attribute" statements.

Calculation of Overall Weighted Values

An overall weighted value for how the OR as it is operating *now* and how it *should* be operating was obtained. And, in a similar vein we obtained an overall weighted value for the court when it was being used to resolve landlord/ tenant disputes, *prior* to the advent of the OR. This was done by taking the numerical utility judgment that each expert gave to the sixteen attributes and multiplying each such utility by the importance weight of the attribute. These weighted utilities were then summed over all attributes. This is the familiar additive rule represented by equation 5. The result can be interpreted as an overall measure of "goodness" or composite utility.

TABLE 16
Average Utilities for Each Value Attribute for the OR Now, How It Should Be, and How It Was Prior to the OR (Court)

Value Attribute	Now	Should	Prior (Court)
Fairness	38.1	76.0	53.1
Impartiality	39.9	76.1	57.1
Accessibility	31.9	55.9	23.6
Education	26.9	47.4	11.7
Visibility	27.6	43.1	20.1
Speed	23.1	43.1	18.4
Power	18.1	37.9	41.5
Expertise	28.6	40.6	27.2
Flexibility	25.0	31.4	22.4
Consistency	20.6	32.5	23.6
Independence	19.5	34.7	29.4
Investigative Power	18.3	32.2	11.4
Jurisdiction	18.4	23.9	25.5
Cost[1]	13.8	25.8	8.9
Informality	12.2	14.6	8.0
Expense[1]	4.5	4.8	4.5

1. The numbers assigned to these attributes were transformed such that the higher the number, the "better," i.e., less cost, less expense.

The results are given in Table 15, which presents the summary statistics for the overall weighted utilities, averaged over all twelve experts. By comparing the overall averages, either mean or median, we see that the OR was considered an improvement on the court, although the differences are not that large. We also note that the averages for the OR utility *should* are always higher than the OR utility *now,* indicating that the experts thought there was room for improvement.

The reason why the court receives an overall weighted utility not too far below that for the OR is that the court receives higher ratings on the attributes of *fairness* and *impartiality,* and these were the attributes that received the highest importance weights (see Table 14). We turn now to a more detailed comparison of the individual attributes.

INDIVIDUAL VALUES FOR EACH ATTRIBUTE

Table 16 presents the results of the averaged utilities for each value attribute for the OR *now,* how it *should* be, and how it was *prior* to the OR (the court). By comparing the OR *now* column with the *prior* (court) column we see that in six of the sixteen attributes, the court receives higher average utilities than the OR. These are for the attributes: *fairness, impar-*

tiality, power (to enforce decisions), *consistency, independence,* and *juris-diction.* For nine of the other attributes, the OR received higher averaged utilities than the court, the attribute of *expense* (to the institution) received the same utility (4.5), indicating the OR and the court were considered equivalent on this particular attribute.

INDIVIDUAL SATISFACTION INDICES

As a final result to be presented we did an analysis of how each individual expert rated the OR on how each importance attribute was being represented in the current operation *(now)* and how it should be represented *(should).* We can state categorically that just about every expert thought the OR could improve on every attribute. Thus, the result is not too interesting and we will not present the data in tabular form. However, a similar analysis on how the OR compared with the court indicated no such unanimity of opinion. For each expert we compared his (her) numerical rating of the OR on each of the attributes with the rating that same expert gave to the court. We were thus able to tabulate how "satisfied" each expert was with respect to the OR versus the court on each attribute and for completeness we included an overall measure of satisfaction. The results are given in Table 17, which depicts the attributes along the columns and the experts along the rows.

A "+" in the body of the table indicates that the expert thought the OR was better than the court on that attribute, and a "−" indicates the converse, i.e., the court was better than the OR on that attribute. A "0" means the expert was neutral on that particular attribute. The results in Table 17 are self-explanatory, but a few things should be pointed out. Note, as indicated by the last column, only two experts thought the court was overall a better way to handle landlord/tenant disputes than the OR was. The other ten experts preferred the OR. On particular attributes, however, the court was considered much better than the OR. The most notable of these is *power* (to enforce a decision) in which not a single expert yielded a "+" for the OR. On other attributes, on the other hand, the OR was considered much better than the court. Examples of these are *accessibility, education, flexibility, investigative power, speed,* and *visibility.* Finally we would like to point out that on the attribute of *expertise,* seven of the experts thought the court was better, three thought the OR was better, and two had no opinion or were neutral.

Comment

The evaluation indicates that overall the OR seems to be working successfully. All save two of the experts concur in this. However, the most

TABLE 17

How Each Expert Compared the Office of the Rentalsman with the Court on the Value Attributes[1]

Expert	Accessibility	Consistency	Cost	Education	Expense	Expertise	Fairness	Flexibility	Impartiality	Independence	Information	Investigative Power	Jurisdiction	Power	Speed	Visibility	Overall Value[2]
1	+	+	−	+	−	+	+	−	0	0	+	+	−	−	+	+	+
2	−	−	−	+	−	−	−	−	−	−	+	−	−	−	−	−	−
3	+	+	+	+	+	+	+	+	+	0	0	+	−	−	+	+	+
4	+	+	−	0	0	0	0	+	−	+	−	+	−	−	+	+	+
5	+	0	+	+	−	0	+	+	−	−	+	+	−	0	+	+	+
6	+	−	+	+	+	−	−	+	+	−	+	+	−	−	+	+	+
7	0	−	0	0	−	+	−	+	−	−	+	+	−	−	+	+	+
8	+	−	0	+	0	−	−	−	+	−	0	+	−	−	−	−	−
9	+	−	+	+	0	−	−	+	−	−	+	0	−	−	+	+	+
10	+	+	+	+	+	+	+	+	0	−	−	+	−	−	0	+	+
11	−	+	+	+	0	−	−	−	+	−	+	0	+	−	+	+	+
12	+	+	+	+	0	−	−	+	+	−	+	+	+	−	+	+	+

1. A "+" means the expert thought the Office of the Rentalsman was better than the Court on that attribute; a "−" means that the expert thought the Court was better on that attribute; a "0" means a neutral or no judgment.

2. The value assigned here is for the overall weighted satisfaction index.

interesting aspect of the evaluation results is the indication of where the operation of the OR can be improved. This is an example of one way to use MAUT to fine tune a program. There were attributes that the experts thought were better handled by the courts, the most prominent of these being *fairness* and *impartiality*, which received the highest importance weights. Also, there is strong evidence that the experts would like to see the OR improve substantially on these two attributes (see Table 16). This is one of the advantages of this particular evaluation technique—it essentially gives a "profile" of the strengths and the weaknesses of a particular social system, in this case the OR. It also indicates a possible dilemma.

In order to improve on the attributes of *fairness* and *impartiality*, the procedural practices of the OR may have to be made more formal, at least for those disputes requiring a hearing. This may mean adopting some of the formal mechanisms of the court that it replaced. Again, the MAUT technique indicates that this is probably desirable since the attribute of *informality* receives the second lowest importance weight of 3.3, which is more than three times lower than the most important attributes of *fairness* and *impartiality*.

Subaggregation

Equation 1 of this chapter suggests that the goal of MAUT is to come up with one number, U, for each object of evaluation, expressing in highly concentrated form how well that object does on all evaluative dimensions.

But whether that much compression is appropriate depends very much on the purpose of the evaluation. Indeed, the discussion of the Office of the Rentalsman example shows that an aggregate was too compressed even in that instance; much of the discussion looked at individual location measures.

It is not too difficult to compare location measures if, as in that example, there are sixteen attributes and two objects of evaluation. But as the numbers of attributes and objects of evaluation increase, the need for aggregation becomes imperative. Fortunately, aggregation need not be an all-or-nothing affair. If a value tree has been developed, one can select an appropriate level of higher-order value, and aggregate up to it. This is done by using equation 5, but starting the process of multiplying the weights down through the tree at the level to which you wish to subaggregate, and thus in effect treating each branch of the tree as a separate MAUT analysis. Then the MAUT scores on each branch separately can be presented as a value profile—an aggregated but still informative summary of how each object of evaluation stands with respect to each of the higher-level values considered relevant to its assessment.

We would illustrate the technique here, but it would be a waste of space to do so. Chapter 7 begins with an example of subaggregation applied to the site selection problem of chapter 2. Each site is characterized by its score on the four top-level attributes of that evaluation—and then further arithmetic is done on those already aggregated scores.

Although the idea of subaggregation has been obvious ever since MAUT came into existence, we know of relatively few instances of its application in program evaluation contexts. That surprises us. The technique seems obvious and appropriate, especially if the purpose of the evaluation is to monitor a program or to guide the process of fine tuning it. The reason, of course, is that it gives information at whatever level of detail seems to be just right for the purpose at hand.

Is it science fictional of us to think that the day might come when every progress report would be accompanied by a subaggregated value profile of the project, with the location measures justified if necessary, and with weights agreed on in advance by sponsor and project people? We know of no other way of compressing information into such a clear and sharp display of exactly what one really wants to know.

Summary

Chapter 6 describes how to aggregate the two sets of numbers arrived at in the MAUT process: the importance weights, one for each attribute, and the location measures (utilities) assigned to each decision alternative on each of the attributes. Only one aggregation rule is presented since research indicates that it is the most practical and useful. The rule: Multiply each location measure on the attribute by the importance weight for that attribute and add up all these products into an aggregate utility U for each decision alternative, entity, or option being evaluated. The larger the numerical value of U, the "better"; thus whatever decision alternative received the largest U should be considered "best" under the procedures described in this document. Two examples are given in detail showing all the calculations. An illustration of how to present an evaluation profile for a program is given. With such a profile it is possible to see the strong and weak points of a program and thus guide the decision maker in deciding where program improvements should be made. The chapter concludes with a discussion of subaggregation of location measures with the appropriate weights. This is done by aggregating the weights and location measures at different levels of the value tree. For example, each branch of the tree can be treated as a separate MAUT analysis. An actual example of subaggregation is left for chapter 7, where it is shown useful for sensitivity analyses of the MAUT procedure.

7. SENSITIVITY ANALYSIS

Sensitivity analysis consists of changing some of the numbers that went into the initial MAUT analysis and doing it over again to see if the conclusions change, and if so, by how much.

Obviously, since the initial calculations of MAUT are demanding, any sensitivity analysis will be more so. Indeed, full-blown sensitivity analyses require more in the way of computational support than this paper assumes to be available. Consequently, we do not plan to illustrate an elaborate sensitivity analysis. Nothing that we propose in this chapter is beyond the capabilities of a hand-held calculator. Even so, we must warn you that this chapter is tedious and hard to read. If you are not doing a MAUT evaluation, skim it. If you are, get paper and pencil and follow the arithmetic.

Probably the most important kind of sensitivity to look at is sensitivity to weights. This is important both because weights are the essence of value judgments, and because weights, being purely subjective numbers about which people disagree, are more likely to be in dispute than location measures, which may be objective, may depend on the judgments of experts-or may be in some cases matters of intense controversy. Moreover, if there is some debate about whether a branch or twig belongs in the analysis at all, it can be in effect eliminated in a sensitivity analysis by giving it a weight of 0, or almost that.

We confine our discussion to the drug counseling center siting example.

Step 1: Subaggregating the Location Measure Matrix

The director, reviewing the original analysis presented in chapter 2, felt that she was satisfied with the choices of twigs used, and with the lower-level weights. While she might have quibbled with some of the latter, she also knew that changes in lower-level weights will have much less impact on aggregate utility than will changes in higher-level weights. This decision permitted a considerable simplification of the analysis.

Her first step was to subaggregate each of the sites to a level just below the top. The result is shown in Table 18. The cost of each site in terms of rent per year is also included in Table 18. The numbers in Table 18 are easy to calculate by hand. Consider the aggregated value of 60.00 for site 1 on Value B. If you refer back to Table 4 (chapter 2), you will find that it is composed of a location measure of 40 for BA and of 80 for BB. The weights of each of these within the B branch (from Figure 1) are .5. So the calculation is .5(40) + .5(80) = 60. Table 19 of this chapter shows how the value of 63.60 for site 1 on branch A was calculated. All other numbers in Table 18 are calculated in the same way.

TABLE 18
Level 1: Subaggregate Utilities of the Six Sites and Cost

Site Number	Attribute Label				Cost (rent per year)
	A	B	C	D	
1	63.60	60.00	32.40	6.40	$48,000
2	48.40	50.00	64.00	59.20	53,300
3	43.90	47.50	13.80	75.60	54,600
4	70.20	50.00	30.80	66.20	60,600
5	35.55	47.50	90.80	35.60	67,800
6	43.30	50.00	46.80	52.80	53,200

The director next inspected this new table of subaggregated location measures for dominance. Of course, 6 is dominated by 2, as before, but otherwise no new dominated sites appear. Some other site could have become dominated at this stage. If its cost (rent) had also been equal to or higher than that of the dominating site, it could be summarily eliminated from further analysis. (Actually, we would eliminate site 6 at this point if we were doing the analysis "for real"; the price difference between it and 2, which dominates it in utility, is so small that 6 has no chance of ending up the winner. We keep it in because it helps to illustrate some important tools later.)

Next, the director noted which sites were best and worst on each top level value, and what the range between minimum and maximum values were for each. The results appear in Table 20.

Step 2: Varying Weights

Inspection of Table 20 told the director that site 5 was most likely to be influenced by the sensitivity analysis—indeed, it could become a top contender if C, with the widest range, were given a high weight. Changing the weight of B was unlikely to make much difference, since the range of variation in B was so small, relative to the other attributes. Changing weights on C and D would make the most difference in ordering of sites. However, D, *administrative convenience,* had originally received a weight of .14, and the director felt that that was plenty. She was most concerned about the weights on A and C. So she decided to change those two weights, holding B and D constant, to see what would happen. (Since the weights must sum to 1, it is impossible to change only one weight.) Since her feeling had initially been that A received too high a weight, she tried only lower weights for A and higher ones for C. Inspection of Tables 18 and 20 told her that such changes would help 2 and 5, and hurt 1 and 4. To make these weight changes, she did not need to go back to the original location measures. Instead, she used Table 18 and applied the weights to those aggregated utilities directly; a simple computational task.

First, she decided to explore a radical change, in which B continued to have a weight of .24 and D a weight of .14, but A had a weight of .23 and C a weight of .39. Next she tried an intermediate change, in which A weighed .33 and C weighed .29. The results of both calculations are shown in Table 21. Now she considered old and new rank orderings in utility. The original rank ordering in aggregate utility (from chapter 2) had been 425163. The first set of weights of Table 21 produces a rank ordering of 524613. The second produces 254613. As expected, the weight changes hurt sites 1 and 4, helped 5 greatly, and helped 2 a little. Inspection of the original location measures or of Table 18 will show why this is so; site 5

TABLE 19

Calculation of a Subaggregated Utility (Site 1, Attribute A)

Twig Label	Location Measure	Weight	Location Measure x Weight
AA	90	.39	63.60
AB	5	.21	10.50
AC	30	.14	4.20
AD	90	.14	12.60
AE	10	.12	1.20
Sums		1.00	63.60

TABLE 20

Best Sites, Worst Sites, and Range for Top-Level Attributes

Attributes	Best Site[1]	Worst Site[1]	Range from Best to Worst
A	4 (70.20)	5 (35.55)	34.65
B	1 (60)	3 & 5 (47.50)	12.50
C	5 (90.80)	3 (13.80)	77.00
D	3 (75.60)	1 (6.40)	69.20

1. The values in the parentheses are the subaggregated utilities from Table 18.

TABLE 21
Result of a Sensitivity Analysis of Changing Weights for Attributes A and C

Site No.	(1) Weights	(2) Weights	Cost
	A = .23	A = .33	
	B = .24	B = .24	
	C = .39	C = .29	
	D = .14	D = .14	
1	42.56	45.68	$48,000
2	56.38	54.82	53,300
3	37.46	40.47	54,600
4	49.43	53.37	60,600
5	59.98	54.45	67,800
6	47.60	47.26	53,200

is outstanding on the twigs under C, but does much less well on most other twigs.

The rank ordering from lowest to highest cost (rent) is 162345. For the original weights, that left sites 1, 2, and 4 as contenders. For the second set of weights (the first in Table 21), the contenders are 1, 2, 5 (highest utility), and 6. Site 4 is now dominated by site 2. For the third set of weights the contenders are 1, 2, and 6; 5 drops out because it is dominated by 2. In both cases 6 remains a contender because of its relatively low cost. We now illustrate another way of depicting which sites are viable contenders. Simply plot the alternatives in a graph relating aggregated utility (Y axis) to the cost (X axis). This is illustrated in Figure 9 for the second set of weights (the first set listed in Table 21: A = .23, B = .24, C = .39, D = .14). Note the line segment connecting sites 1, 2, and 5. These are clearly the best sites and even though 6 remains in contention because of its low cost, it will not survive. This is a general property of such plots. Any sites in this example that fall below the concave line segment will be eliminated. The converse is also true. Any new alternative plotted on or above the curve would become a contender. Depending on its location, it could cause previous contenders now to be dominated.

At this point, the director would like to know whether the intermediate possibilities for these two new sets of weights are realistic contenders in view of the relation between cost and utility. Consider first the second set of weights (the first set listed in Table 21). For this set of weights, she needs to prepare a table similar to Table 7 in chapter 2. Table 22 shows successive differences for the four potential contenders in both utility and cost (the arithmetic is the same as that performed in Table 7). Set the utility and cost difference for the top site to 0. Then subtract from each site's

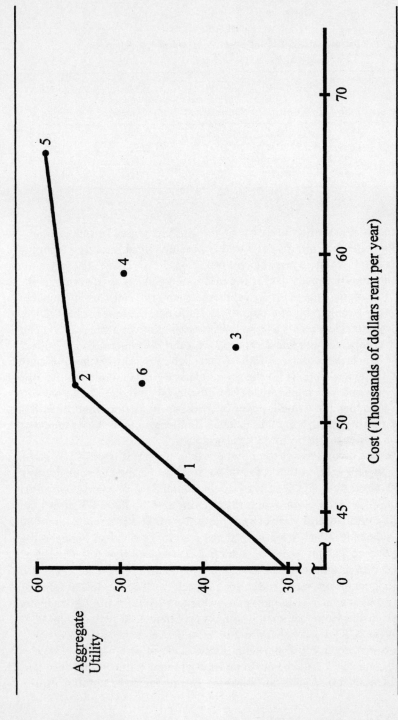

Figure 9: Graphic Representation of Utility Versus Cost (weights: A = .23; B = .24; C = .39; D = .14)

87

TABLE 22
Increments in Utilities and Costs, Sites 1, 2, 5, and 6
(weights: A = .23; B = .24; C = .39; D = .14)

Site No.	Utility	Cost	Utility Differences (Incremental)	Cost Differences (Incremental)	Cost Incr./ Utility Incr.
1	42.56	$48,000	0	0	
6	47.60	53,200	5.04	$5200	$1032
2	56.38	53,300	8.78	100	11
5	59.98	67,800	3.60	14500	4027

utility and cost the utility and cost of the site just above it. For example, the utility difference of 5.04 for site 6 is obtained by subtracting from the utility of site 1, which is just above it (47.60 - 42.56 = 5.04). These are the increments in utility and cost for the undominated sites. Inspection of the ratio of cost increments to utility increments for site 2 tells us at once that something is wrong. A bit of thought makes the nature of the problem clear. Obviously, site 6 represents a large increment in cost for a small increment in utility compared with site 2. That is why the ratio increment for site 2 is so low. You may recall from Table 7 that such ratios should continuously increase in such a table, if all the contenders are true contenders. In this case they do not. The implication (which is in fact a theorem that we will not prove) is that site 6 could never be chosen, no matter what the dollar value of a utility point, from these sites with these weights. Consequently, it is not a contender, and should be eliminated.

Although a quick look at the numbers tells us that it is unlikely, and a look at Figure 9 tells us that it is not so, it could be the case considering Table 22 alone that site 2 is also not a contender. To check, we must calculate Table 22 all over again, eliminating site 6. Table 23 shows the result. As expected, this check simply confirms that 2 is a real contender. It also makes clear that, even with these weights, the range between the dollar value of a utility point for which 2 is best and that for which 5 is best is very large indeed. (Note that Table 22 could not have been used to reach this conclusion, since it did not properly reflect the dollar value of a utility point at which 2 becomes preferable to 1.) With Table 23, we know that if the dollar value per utility point is less than $383, site 1 is best. If it is between $383 and $4027, site 2 is best. If over $4027, site 5 is best.

Since 6 was also a contender with the third set of weights (A = .33, C = .29), the same check must be made on its contender status in that case also (Table 24 does so). Again the numbers in the far right column do not

TABLE 23

Increments in Utilities and Costs, Sites 1, 2, and 5

(weights: A = .23; B = .24; C = .39; D = .14)

Site No.	Utility Differences (Incremental)	Cost Differences (Incremental)	Cost Incr./ Utility Incr.
1	0	0	
2	13.82	$5300	$383
5	3.60	14500	4027

increase steadily. And again option 6 should be deleted. In this case, there is no point in redoing Table 24 without site 6 in it to make sure that 1 and 2 are contenders, since the best in utility (site 2) and the lowest in cost (site 1) will always be contenders. It is, however, useful to know what the value of a utility point is for which 2 becomes better than 1 with these new weights—and Table 24 does not tell us that. Table 25 does. If the value of a utility point is more than $580, then with these weights site 2 is preferable to site 1.[3]

In the original analysis of chapter 2, 4 had been better than 2, though substantially more expensive. At this point, it becomes interesting to see for what values of the weights of A and C (holding the weights of B and D constant) 2 and 4 become equal in utility. From Table 18 of this chapter, the larger the weight of A relative to C, the better 4 will do compared with 2. So a weight of A higher than .33 is needed. Trial and error (or solution of a simple linear equation) shows that .36 does the trick. However, even if the weight of A were higher than .36, a second look at Table 7 will remind you that with the weights used in that chapter, 2 was still preferable to 4 over a wide range of the dollar values of a utility point. The director combined that fact with her own feeling that the weight of A should not be greater than .36—a feeling that she also checked with her contract monitor, who agreed. So she narrowed the set of contenders down to 1 and 2.

Step 3: Varying Location Measures

This led her to reexamine the location measures for 1 and 2. (With more computational resources, she might have done a more extensive examination of the measures.) She was particularly concerned with twig CA, the location measures describing the suitability of the individual treatment rooms. This was a judgment combining their number, their suitability to their function, their convenience of location to the waiting room, their

TABLE 24
Increments In Utilities and Costs, A = .33, Sites 1, 2, and 6
(weights: A = .23; B = .24; C = .39; D = .14)

Site No.	Utility Differences (Incremental)	Cost Differences (Incremental)	Cost Incr./ Utility Incr.
1	0	0	
6	1.58	$5200	$3294
2	7.6	100	13

attractiveness, and so on. Even with a weight of .19 for branch C, CA still receives a weight of .10 (see Figure 1 in chapter 2), which made it the most important of the judgmental C-branch twigs. Both BA and BB got higher weights, but she was quite content with her assessment of them. Moreover, sites 1 and 2 differed radically on CA; 1 got a location measure of 10, and 2 got one of 80. They differed little on BA and BB (see Table 4 in chapter 2). She decided to see how much she would need to change the location measures for CA in order to make sites 1 and 2 equal in utility. She of course had to pick a set of upper level weights for the calculation, and chose to use the one in which branch C had a weight of .29. With that upper level weight for C, the twig weight for CA is .29 × .50 = .151. The utility difference between 1 and 2, for that set of weights, is 9.14. So she would need a change in the location measure for CA of 9.14/.151 = 60.5 to make 1 and 2 equal in utility with that set of weights. She quickly concluded that, though she was less secure about that judgment than about some of the others, she could not possibly have been 60 points off. She did not see any need to repeat previous calculations with new locations for CA. Site 5 already scored very high on it (90), and site 4, though lower (50), was not so low that it would make a substantial difference to the outcome.

A final step, more from curiosity than because she considered it crucial, she performed the computationally very easy task of trying equal weights. First she tried weighting equally all the original location measures (from chapter 2). After doing so, she eliminated dominated sites, and found that sites 5, 2, 6, and 1 were left. Further checking showed, as before, that although site 6 was undominated, it could never be chosen. The utility difference between 2 and 5 was only 2.5 utility points, and the price per utility point that made 5 preferable to 2 was $5,800—a very high price per utility point indeed for this example. Next, she weighted equally the sub-aggregated utilities of Table 18. The dominance analysis left her with sites 1, 6, and 2, in order of increasing utility. And, as usual, site 6 dropped out because any price per utility point that would make it better than 1 would

TABLE 25
Increments in Utilities and Costs, Sites 1 and 2
(weights: A = .33; B = .24; C.29; D = .14)

Site No.	Utility Differences (Incremental)	Cost Differences (Incremental)	Cost Incr./ Utility Incr.
1	0	0	
2	9.14	5300	580

make 2 better than it. In both of these analyses, the price per utility point that would make 2 preferable to 1 was modest: $578 in the first case and $358 in the second. These findings strengthened her already strong feeling not only that site 2 was her best choice, but also that that choice was stable under a variety of different weights.

Step 4: Choosing the Final Form of the Analysis

After this (somewhat abbreviated) sensitivity analysis, she invited members of the staff who wished to do so to try their own weights on the contending sites, repeating the analyses already presented. None led to substantially different results. She then decided that she would recommend site 2 to her sponsors and to the other stakeholders. The set of weights that she most believed, and that she based the recommendation on, was the one for which A was weighted .33 and C was weighted .29. Inspection of Table 21 shows that sites 1 and 2 differ by 9.14 utility points and by $5,300 in price. You will recall from Table 25 that for this set of weights the value of a utility point in dollars for which 2 becomes preferable to 1 is $580. To convince herself and others that a utility point was at least that valuable, she included examples like those presented in chapter 2 in which stakeholders are asked to judge the value of a 100-point swing in a twig. Twig DA (with a weight of .09) was used as the example in chapter 2. The new weights do not affect that twig, since the weight of D remains unchanged. So a 100-point swing in DA is still a change of 9 points in aggregate utility. (That number would have changed if a twig under the B or the C branch had been chosen for the example.) For any value greater than $5,220 (9 × 580) of a 100-point swing in DA, a point of utility is worth more than $580. None of her stakeholders was reluctant to agree that such a swing was worth at least that much. So she recommended site 2.

Her recommendation was accepted—in part because it was bolstered by such a thorough analysis of the available alternatives to it.

Generalizations About Sensitivity Analysis

The preceding paragraphs imply some generalizations about sensitivity analysis. The first and most important is that careful inspection of the original numbers, and of compressions of them like Table 18 serve to guide exploration; there is no reason to try computations at random.

The second generalization is that if a number of options are to be examined, it is usually desirable and feasible to reduce that number considerably, thus confining the sensitivity analysis to a much smaller set of options and so reducing arithmetic. Dominance permits this to be done formally. But even without dominance, it is usually possible to recognize options to be dropped. Although we did not do it, it is obvious from Table 18 that, unless the weight of administrative convenience (D) is allowed to go much higher than the director felt was reasonable, site 3 should have been summarily dropped. Every option dropped reduces the arithmetical labor of doing a sensitivity analysis, and so permits a more careful job to be done. Note, however, that utility dominance is not in itself an adequate basis for dropping options, if they are cheap. Site 6 remained in contention almost to the end. This is essentially an accident of this example. Site 2 is so close to site 6 in price that it would have been sensible to drop site 6 intuitively. As it turns out, a final analysis that included sites 1, 2, 4, and 5 would have captured everything that the director (though not the readers of this paper) would need to know.

Obviously, weight sensitivity should be looked at first. Usually, it is enough to work only with the higher-level weights, since the lower-level ones have so much less effect. It is also computationally more convenient. The device, illustrated by Table 18, of aggregating weights and location measures up to the level just below the one at which the sensitivity analysis is to be done, will make the arithmetic easier.

Since there are so many location measures in any MAUT analysis, it is not easy or straightforward to figure out which ones to vary in a sensitivity analysis. The obvious guides are (1) that it makes little sense to vary location measures on low-weighted twigs, (2) that it is equally inappropriate to vary location measures that do not discriminate among the viable contenders unless there is some reason to believe that one of them is wrong, and (3) that one should think hard about which locations one trusts, and which are dubious. Without more computational aid than we can offer, exploration of changing location measures is likely to be perfunctory.

For situations such as that examined in this document, in which both utility and cost are often relevant, calculation of cost per utility point implied by choice of each undominated option is an indispensable adjunct to analysis based on utilities alone. Formally, these techniques amount to bringing cost in as another attribute of the utility function. We have chosen to treat cost and utility separately until the end of the analysis in this volume because in many evaluation situations choice among options on the basis of both utility and cost is not the issue—though in many others it is. Consequently, we wanted to provide both methods for dealing with utility alone and methods for combining utility with cost. This chapter has abundantly illustrated how inclusion of cost considerations can affect choices that, in their absence, would be based on utility alone, and has offered methods for exploring the sensitivity of the evaluation process to cost even in the absence of the judgments that establish direct relationships between utility points and dollars. That is because such judgments are often particularly hard to make, and are likely to be more controversial than other judgments that enter into the evaluation process. Fortunately, as this chapter has suggested, rather crude assessments of the value of a utility point will often permit a clear-cut choice after dominated options have been eliminated.

No one has yet discovered rules that guide one in making simultaneous changes of the many numbers in a sensitivity analysis. Even with extensive computer support, such large-scale sensitivity analyses are often confusing and frustrating. If the conclusion seems to be relatively stable under changes of weights, as it was in this example, you are usually justified in treating it as valid.

That is how the result will usually turn out. Even in this example, which was designed to be sensitive to weights and turned out to be so much so that we originally wondered whether we had not chosen a poor example, the finding in favor of site 2 ends up seeming quite stable, given a willingness to spend some extra rent for more utility. You are unlikely to encounter a real case more weight-sensitive than this one.

If you do, it will be for one or the other or both of two reasons. One is that two or more options are so close in aggregated utility that it makes virtually no difference which is picked, and so changes in weight switch them back and forth in ranking. This is essentially what happened to sites 2, 4, and 5 of this example. In that kind of situation, other attributes not included in the original analysis should be considered, since the original analysis led to what amounts to a tie. In this analysis, the additional attribute was cost. The other reason for sensitivity to weights is that the options, instead of being relatively homogeneous in location measures like site 2, include many very high and very low ones like site 5. Obviously the larger the range of variation of location within an option, the greater the sensitivity to weights will be. Only in this case do we feel that real precision in knowing weights is indispensable. And, in our real world experience, such instances are relatively rare, though they do occur.

A final comment. We have said very little about uncertainty about weights or measures. Locations that depend on judgment are likely to vary depending both on who does the judging and on when and how the number is elicited. While we do pay attention to the magnitude of utility differences in considering whether a utility difference is worth what it costs or not, we do not otherwise pay much attention to such variability. The reason is simply that when a decision must be made, you work with what you have. It makes no difference whether a difference is "significant" in some statistical sense or not. If it is the best guidance you have about what option to choose, you should follow it. And if it is not, then you will be able to incorporate whatever additional guidance you may be able to get into an expanded multiattribute utility analysis. You always leave attributes out to keep the analysis simple. If an analysis leaves you uncomfortably uncertain about what to do or think, and if the problem is important enough to justify another iteration, you can always go back, include more value attributes, reweight, reaggregate, and repeat the analysis. Or, as occasionally happens, if the formal analysis leaves several options very close together in attractiveness, you may choose to consider other attributes informally. This is highly appropriate if they all point in the same direction. If not, then they present you with the kind of trade-off problem for which MAUT is intended, and an expanded version of the formal analysis becomes the method of choice.

Summary

Chapter 7 is concerned with an analysis of the MAUT technique itself. It attempts to determine just how sensitive the final result of MAUT is to the numbers and arithmetic that went into the analysis. Sensitivity analysis typically consists of a series of steps. Step 1 consists of subaggregation in which the overall utility of each entity being evaluated is recalculated at higher branches of the value tree. Step 2 consists of varying the importance weights on the main branches of the tree involved in the subaggregation. At this stage the effects of dropping value attributes can also be investigated by the simple process of assigning a weight of zero to any attribute one wishes to eliminate. Step 3 consists of changing the utilities.

The selection of a drug counseling site, first introduced in Chapter 2, is used to illustrate all the arithmetic. With the subaggregated utilities further aggregated using different weights, it is now possible to check again for dominance, i.e., to see if any sites can be eliminated because better and cheaper sites exist. For any change made in the conduct of a sensitivity analysis the result is always compared with the original MAUT result to see if any major changes take place in the final choice. Often, the final choice is not changed drastically by such changes. When this happens, as it often does in practice, one can have confidence in the MAUT analysis. If this does not happen, i.e., if relatively minor changes in the inputs to

MAUT yield quite different results, then the MAUT analysis may need expansion.

NOTES

1. Attribute 6, Option 1 in Table 2 shows a value of 105 on a 0-100 scale. This simply means that the project director judged 1981 performance on this dimension to be better than the best he thought could be expected when he defined endpoints of the dimension. While such violations of the 0-100 range can occur, they should be rare.

2. Much of the material in this chapter was prepared by Dave Seaver and Kurt Snapper of Maxima, Inc.

3. Footnote for technicians only: The tools based on successive differences presented in this section of this chapter serve two purposes. First, they identify any points that lie in concave portions of the function relating aggregate utility to cost, and eliminate them. Second, for the convex function that remains, they identify the critical slopes, or trade-off relations between aggregate utility and money, for which preferences switch from one option to the next. These tools seem to us simpler and more precise than their graphic counterparts such as Figure 9. If the x-axis were treated as the utility of money rather than money itself, the tools of this chapter would be general. This, of course, assumes that the weighted additive utility function holds.

REFERENCES

EDWARDS, W. (1980) "Multiattribute utility for evaluation: Structures, uses, and problems," in M. Klein and K. Teilmann (eds.) *Handbook of criminal justice evaluation.* Beverly Hills, CA: Sage.
——— (1977) "How to use multiattribute utility measurement for social decision making." *IEEE Transactions on Systems, Man, and Cybernetics 7:* 326-340.
——— (1971) "Social utilities." *Engineering Economist 6:* 119-129.
——— A. M. GUTTENTAG, and K. SNAPPER (1975) "Effective evaluation: A decision theoretic approach," in C. A. Bennett and A. Lumsdaine (eds.) *Evaluation and experiment: Some critical issues in assessing social programs.* New York: Academic.
KLEIN, M. and K. TEILMANN [eds.] (1980) *Handbook of criminal justice evaluation.* Beverly Hills, CA: Sage.
SNAPPER, K. and D. SEAVER (1978) *Application of decision analysis to program planning and evaluation,* Technical Report 78-1. Reston, VA: Decision Science Consortium, Inc.

SUPPLEMENTARY REFERENCES

EIHORN, B. and R. M. HOGARTH (1975) "Unit weighting schemes for decision making." *Organizational Behavior and Human Performance 13:* 171-192.
KEENEY, R. and H. RAIFFA (1976) *Decisions with multiple objectives: Preferences and value tradeoffs.* New York: John Wiley.
NEWMAN, J. R. (1977) "Differential weighting in a multiattribute utility measurement: When it should not and when it does make a difference." *Organizational Behavior and Human Performance 20:* 312-325.

ABOUT THE AUTHORS

WARD EDWARDS is Professor of Psychology and Industrial & Systems Engineering and Director of the Social Science Research Institute, University of Southern California. He obtained a Ph.D. in experimental psychology from Harvard in 1952, and has taught at Johns Hopkins University, the University of Michigan, and the University of Southern California. He has written many articles and books in the fields of behavioral decision theory and decision analysis. His current research focuses on use of multiattribute utility methods to understand and alleviate social conflicts produced by the introduction of new and possibly hazardous technologies.

J. ROBERT NEWMAN is Professor of Psychology, California State University at Long Beach, and Senior Research Associate, Social Science Research Institute, University of Southern California. He holds a Ph.D. in psychology from the University of Illinois. Professor Newman is the author of numerous articles in scientific journals and has conducted several program evaluation studies on criminal and civil justice systems. He is currently applying decision analysis techniques to medical diagnosis and treatment decisions.

Printed in the United States
50806LVS00007B/55-69